JUKE JOINTS, JAZZ CLUBS & JUICE

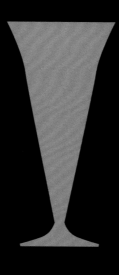

JUKE JOINTS, JAZZ CLUBS & JUICE

COCKTAILS FROM TWO CENTURIES *of* AFRICAN AMERICAN COOKBOOKS

TONI TIPTON-MARTIN

Photographs by Brittany Conerly

CLARKSON POTTER/PUBLISHERS

NEW YORK

To my husband, Bruce Martin,
whose preference is for good bourbon,
just poured over an ice ball

CONTENTS

⁝⁝⁝⁝⁝

INTRODUCTION

:::::

Heaven and Earth have always loved wine,
so how could loving wine shame heaven?

—Li Po, translated by Kevin Young

I don't drink cocktails and the only one I know how to make
is a Molotov, and I'd be a fool to give the recipe here.

—Vertamae Smart-Grosvenor

It is early morning in January and the ground outside my window is covered by a blanket of fresh-fallen snow. The birds are chirping as they bounce from one branch to another in the gracious fig tree just beyond the porch. It is cold and the birds are searching for food. I am warming up with a hot cup of hibiscus and rose hip tea in the parlor that is now my cookbook library, a cozy room where the windows are a lens into another world. I love this space.

It is much too early for my thoughts to be rambling between cocktails and the seasonal harvest, but here I am envisioning the voluptuous fruit that will appear on the fig tree and wondering what recipes I should make to preserve their sweet flavor. Not jam.

After a short glance at the bookshelves, over the single-subject books on topics ranging from appetizers to soups, past the American regional books, the recipes by celebrity chefs, and the volumes that explore global flavors, my gaze returns to the beverage section.

I flip through the pages of the scholarly food and history works. Now I am even more distracted. I notice that there are only a few mentions of African Americans and their roles in American mixology. The boozy, syrupy-sweet, fruit-laced libations of the Caribbean are conspicuously missing from the official bartender's guides to mixed drinks. This does not surprise me.

Many years ago, the persistent marginalizing of my ancestors' contributions to American foodways motivated me to collect Black cookbooks to hear firsthand what my people had to say about their cooking. I spent two decades buying and studying our recipe collections—from handmade stapled booklets to spiralbound church and community books to colorful trade-published works. I brought some of these authors forth and explained why their recipes and writings matter in my previous books, *The Jemima Code: Two Centuries of African American Cookbooks* and *Jubilee: Recipes from Two Centuries of African American Cooking.* But as I think about these books while I sip from my cup, their words leave me with a contradiction: Drinking is good; drinking is bad.

Throughout history, African American alcohol consumption has been portrayed as derelict. Advertisements, film and photo images, literature, and scholarship singled out our drunken displays, disparaged our women as "loose" with low morals, and established a temperance movement based on the fear that African Americans would destroy "civil society" with their imbibing.

A photo series published by magazine and newspaper photographer Marion Post Wolcott is just one example of the messaging—the "code," as I have called it. *Negroes gambling with their cotton money in a juke joint outside of Clarksdale, Mississippi Delta* is one of more than 9,000 images she took for the Farm Security Administration (FSA) from 1938 to 1942, while traveling across the country to document and publicize the effect of the Great Depression and agricultural blight. Some of the images imply that African Americans are irresponsible folk who frivolously drink and party their hard-earned incomes away.

It is true that juke joints existed on the edges of agricultural communities. They were, among other things, a place to escape the chronic cruelty of life in a segregated society. In these places, dancing and laughter soothed spirits that ached from the body-and-spirit-breaking labor of picking cotton and cleaning toilets for families with better things to do. At the same time, images of genteel and upstanding white drinkers in taverns, inns, grog shops, billiard clubs, gentlemen's clubs, and bars incurred little scrutiny.

It's no wonder W. E. B. Du Bois, E. Franklin Frazier, Lawrence Otis Graham, and others expressed concerns about proper behavior among Black people and conflated alcohol consumption with the lower class. Stereotyped portrayals of lazy and loose working-class people drunk on bootleg liquor, moonshine, and bathtub gin persist today in sharp contrast to the prestige associated with middle- and upper-class living by Black professionals. It's a dynamic that fosters moralizing, tsk-tsking, and judgment from white and Black people alike.

Historian Arturo Schomburg observed a similar dual-identity theory to discussions of African American foodways in the late 1930s. He wrote but never published a cookbook outline that divided our recipes into two categories: the cooking of the working class and the cooking of the privileged class.

Intrigued by this idea, I looked into his theories on these two pathways in my collection of Black cookbooks, which informed my own cookbook, *Jubilee: Recipes from Two Centuries of African American Cooking*. *Jubilee* identifies and celebrates African American kitchen wisdom as it exists among food professionals, people who had access to quality ingredients and kitchen tools, whether they performed their craft in plantation kitchens, in restaurants, in professional test kitchens, or in private homes—someone else's or their own.

Juke Joints, Jazz Clubs, and Juice picks up where *Jubilee* left off, taking a closer look at the long story of African American mixology traditions, innovations, and craftsmanship.

This project revisits my Black cookbook collection to establish a pedigree for our cocktails that can be traced through published recipes—a history that goes back centuries. It does not try to establish a complete canon. Nor does it explore the rich history of alcohol consumption in America or the history of mixed drinks. For more on those subjects, I recommend the work of David Wondrich, Robert Moss, Robert Simonson, Mallory O'Meara, Sarah Hand Meacham, Kathleen Purvis, Matthew Rowley, and the good folks at the Southern Foodways Alliance.

In *Juke Joints, Jazz Clubs, and Juice,* I have recorded old formulas that have been reimagined and sometimes renamed by African Americans for generations. These are libations that still appear on our menus today. My ambition is to ensure that African American workers who plied their trade behind the bar are not forgotten.

The story unfolds as a collection of spirits, combinations, locales, venues, and iconic characters, and a lineage that we can trace through African American cookbooks published as far back as 1827, with beverage-making history that goes all the way back to the Motherland. The legacy begins with the rich tradition of fermented or brewed beverages made by African women to express hospitality. It identifies New World drinks fermented to cure ailments and distilled to relieve the broken spirits of the enslaved. And it records recipes created by pioneering free people of color who served the public in boardinghouses, taverns, hotels, inns, and grog-shops. Caterers who mixed drinks for guests, and behind-the-bar masters who built reputations for their craft cocktails, are represented here as well. So are the home cooks, educators, and socialites who published cookbooks filled with recipes for mixed drinks to welcome guests into their homes.

Atholene Peyton is the first of those educators to author a recipe book that also asserts bartending expertise. Her collection, *The Peytonia Cook Book,* published in 1906, features tested recipes, including a mint and a pineapple julep; several punches, such as claret, sherry, rum, Roman, and Champagne; two fizzes—gin fizz and society fizz—eggnog; homemade cordials and wine; plus whiskey cocktails like the Whiskey Sour and the Manhattan.

The book features illustrations she drew herself, menus for family tables and special occasions, plus lessons in economy to provide a strong foundation for aspiring cooks. And I believe it should be seen as part of the movement of community-focused women being liberated from the concept of themselves as objects of prejudice, injustice, and brutality to face new horizons of self-awareness, personal pride, and Black consciousness. Peyton dedicated her project to the Women's Clubs of America, a group that championed women's rights. Nannie Helen Burroughs, a member of the Auxiliary to the National Baptist Convention and founding president of the National Training School for Women and Girls in Washington, DC, wrote the preface.

Elegant A-to-Z cocktail compendiums by early mixologists Tom Bullock (1917) and Julian Anderson (1919) follow Peyton. Each book glistens with graceful and quirky titles, trusted combinations, and sweet modifications of cocktail classics; I lean on them heavily, and you will see their inspiration in these pages. And in the post-Prohibition years, caterers Helen Mahammitt and Rebecca West add generous listings for classic cocktails to their cookbooks.

After that, however, bar drinks barely dapple the beverage chapters in Black recipe books. Freda DeKnight's 1948 *A Date with a Dish,* for instance, limits the conversation to spiked café au lait, eggnog, and cooking with wine. In fact, Black booze amplitude essentially fades from our cookbooks during the 1950s with the spirited libations of old disappearing like drops of dew in the early morning sun. Published recipes reappear during the soul food era of the 1960s, with authors focused on the Old South's survival beverages, such as fermented wines, moonshine, and zero-proof drinks like lemonade, sweet tea, and red punches.

Today, though, Black mixology writing is back in style.

Shannon Mustipher's *Tiki: Modern Tropical Cocktails*, for example, debunks clichéd notions of rum as the basis of sticky sweet, Caribbean-resort drinks accented with little paper umbrellas. The spirits educator, cocktail consultant, and rum expert changes the rum drinks game with craft cocktails based on quality spirits, fresh ingredients, and handcrafted syrups.

And if Mustipher represents excellence in modern mixology, *Can I Mix You a Drink? 50 Cocktails from My Life & Career* signals a mixology jubilee. Published in 2021 by Grammy award-winning hip-hop artist T-Pain, this curated collection of "dranks" spins a loose, party vibe, dismantling the narrow perspective that Black mixology history is limited to dapper, anonymous barmen creating amazing cocktails for white country club members. These are just two of a cadre of Black mixology books, or Black cookbooks that feature mixed drinks.

Whether published then or now, each of these important works shares a love of libations and hospitality while adding context to the techniques and knowledge possessed by African American barmasters and the mixes they created that were once considered "unorthodox." Tips, tricks, and inspiration from all of these creative mixmasters are featured on the pages of this book.

I observed the African American tradition of imbibing as an act of hospitality as a young child, maybe 7 or 8, at home in Los Angeles. Whether the occasion was a backyard barbecue or a card party, my mother set up a buffet of food and drink in our walkout basement. She positioned food stations around the pool table that stood regally in the center of the den (the area we sometimes call the family room today). Drinks were served from the bar Dad built himself and from my grandmother Nannie's "Hide-a-Bed" bar cabinet, which held a twin-size fold-out and their glassware, including a brightly colored set of tall, frosted Blendo Collins glasses rimmed with gold, and her Popeye the Sailor glass liquor decanter.

And yet, this is not a highly personal book. I did not come to this subject because of a lifelong passion for imbibing. For many years, my cocktail-making experience was limited to recipes developed in *The Los Angeles Times* and *The Plain Dealer* test kitchens, where cooking was the priority. I clipped recipes for party foods like blue cheese wafers, chicken liver pâté, ceviche, or guacamole and stored them in clear plastic sleeves in a three-ring binder with a few compatible cocktails. The list was short: Champagne cocktail, frozen margarita, and a boozy sangria printed on purple paper, distributed during an International Association of Culinary Professionals (IACP) conference in 2005. For years, I ladled that same pretty red drink with sliced citrus and assorted berries floating on top from my grandmother Nannie's cut-glass punch bowl for Mother's Day brunch, or in tall Collins glasses at summer barbecues.

My repertoire grew a little more when I was invited to cater a series of intimate dinner parties. My son Brandon, a classically trained bartender, helped me pair cocktails with my cultural menus. He shook chocolate martinis to celebrate Valentine's Day, stirred Sazeracs for Mardi Gras, and built hibiscus cocktails to honor freedom during Fourth of July and Juneteenth dinners. The experience motivated me to craft and expand my reliable mixed drink selection, one I could make my own to set an even warmer welcome table.

But to understand modern mixology trends, I first needed to understand the formulas left behind in my ancestors' cookbooks. Like a treasure map through time and locale, recipes from two hundred years of Black libations reveal the drinks my ancestors made regularly—whether they were fermenting wines and cordials from fruit and berries, ladling punches in large batches, or mixing classics built in the glass, layered, shaken, or stirred to perfection.

After a lot of experimenting, I invited next-generation barmasters—Brandon, and Tiffanie Barriere, the Drinking Coach—to teach me the soul of the craft: when I added too much mixer or not enough, stirred when I should have shaken, or bruised the mint instead of muddling it. From them, I learned the number of times one shakes a Martini and for how long, the best type of ice for highballs—and what exactly *is* a highball—and when to choose a light or dark spirit. They walked me through the foundation upon which modern African American cocktails have been built, a tradition that sometimes demands more sweetener than you might expect, and in the case of the old-school masters, more mixing theatrics. They made me thirsty for more knowledge, more skill, and more to drink. I hope you will feel the same after exploring these pages.

ABOUT THE RECIPES AND THE CHAPTERS

I followed classic recipe development processes to help me decide whether a drink should be included in *Juke Joints, Jazz Clubs, and Juice*. The process, which involves researching a recipe's background, testing its methods over and over, recording observations, and translating those findings so anyone can re-create it, is the same formula I followed in *Jubilee*.

First, I scoured my cookbooks for beverages that may have been published years ago but remained popular over time—some to this day. Next, I tested the recipes by comparing the traditional version of a single drink with those published in Black cookbooks through the years. When I figured out which adaptation I liked best, I did some tinkering.

It was important for the drinks to be accessible to everyone, so I made them with readily available ingredients and a few inexpensive bar tools. Most recipes yield one or two servings, but they double easily for those occasions when you want to accommodate additional guests. I also included the original recipe, or the recipe that inspired me, along with my updated version whenever possible so you receive the invitation to imbibe in a language and style that is both ancestral and my own.

I organized the beverages somewhat chronologically and by the technique of the craft, not the spirit. That made some chapters longer than others, but I wanted to share everything I learned after reading, testing, and tasting all of that Black drink history. For example, the number of shaken cocktails is double the number of homemade fermented beverages because so much of the history of our drink preferences during enslavement has been lost or misrepresented. You'll also notice that the essays introducing each chapter and the recipe headnotes are dotted with names, dates, and some social context to help place each drink along that chronological timeline.

In Chapter 1, I invite you to brew beer, ferment wine, and make your own cordials with tales of enslaved and free Black women who created beverage enterprises to earn freedom or some degree of financial security during the antebellum years. I decided that the story of Black caterers and food entrepreneurs told in Chapter 2 was a logical mate for punch bowl drinks and beverages mixed in large batches to serve a crowd. And building a drink in a glass without stirring or shaking seemed like a natural companion to the stories in Chapter 3, which describe the self-reliant, independent-thinking tavern owners of the eighteenth century who made a way for themselves in harsh environments with little support.

After that, the drinks get more playful and sometimes sweeter. Artfully mixed and named after people, places, and even body parts, they arrange themselves into themes. Chapter 4's layered drinks, which bartenders skillfully mixed at private clubs and resorts in service to wealthy guests, mostly white men, expand our thinking about artistry, craftsmanship, and camaraderie at the turn of the twentieth century. And the linkages I draw between the jazz era and shaken cocktails in Chapter 5 is based purely on my theory that bartenders in jazz clubs would have enjoyed the theatrics of shaking and passing drinks overhead from one shaker to the other while dancing girls kicked up their heels and well-dressed audiences sipped their magical mixtures.

In Chapter 6, I contemplate drinks stirred in a more subdued manner in rural juke joints in the woods. Here, booze wasn't a celebration, it was a salve. Finally, Chapter 7 is a meditation on a concept that snuck up on me, namely that Black folks made the choice to drink liquor—or not—as an expression of self-empowerment.

So: Come. On. In. The bar is open!

FERMENTED, BREWED & STEEPED

Ancestral Traditions

ANCESTRAL TRADITIONS

*We got thoroughly dirty playing in the barnyard and miserably
scratched picking wild strawberries, blackberries, plums and possum
grapes (as Grandpa called them), so that Grandmother could make her
jams and jellies—and best of all, her exquisite wines.*

—*Cleora Butler,* Cleora's Kitchens: The Memoir of a Cook, *1985*

Before there was refrigeration, there was the root cellar, a storage place buried
in the cool, damp ground or in the basement where families stashed jars
of homemade pickles, preserved fruits, canned vegetables, and fruited vinegars, a guarantee that the tastes (and nutrients) of summer lasted all winter long.
Many also held a crock or two of homemade hard drink—corn liquor or wine or
brews made with fruit picked from orchards or gardens, gathered from the wild,
or saved from discarded leftovers, such as peach pits, rotting apples, or even carrot
and potato peelings.

Until recently, most American history limited this legacy to images of bootleg-
ging mountain or enslaved Black men working illicit stills in remote corners of the
woods. While this is indeed part of the African American beverage story, it is not
the only part.

We now know that enslaved and free Black women earned freedom or some
degree of financial security for themselves and loved ones during the antebellum
years by creating beverage enterprises from very small plots of land. A woman
named Sally Scott owned an orchard in Virginia, where she established a vineyard
and produced 130 gallons of wine in one year, as Juliet E. K. Walker explains in
The History of Black Business in America: Capitalism, Race, Entrepreneurship. And in
1808, Patsy Young, a 16-year-old with a "bright" complexion, fled to freedom and
made a life for herself in North Carolina by brewing beer, according to research
unearthed by Theresa McCulla, curator with the Smithsonian's American Brewing
History Initiative at the National Museum of American History.

During Prohibition, Bertie "Birdie" Brown, the only African American woman known to be homesteading alone in Montana, built a reputation for the hospitality extended in her parlor. She offered locals and travelers food and comfortable lodging and brewed what locals called the "best moonshine in the country." Today, Saint Liberty Bertie's Bear Gulch Straight Bourbon Whiskey, a triple-pot-distilled whiskey made in Austin, Texas, is keeping Bertie's legacy alive, while innovative chefs, like James Beard award-winner Mashama Bailey, carry on ancestral distilling traditions, as seen in her experiments with ribbon cane shine.

Black cookbooks also reveal African American knowledge and expertise in home brewing and

> We now know that enslaved and free Black women earned freedom or some degree of financial security for themselves and loved ones during the antebellum years by creating beverage enterprises from very small plots of land.

wine making, as well as recipes for invigorating beverages, crafted as far back as the fifteenth century for medicinal purposes, such as herbed cordials and fruit syrups.

"Who didn't make some kind of spirit drink in Chatham County?" Mildred Council, the celebrated North Carolina soul food chef, asked in *Mama Dip's Kitchen.* "People made locust beer, home brew, corn wine, tomato wine, muscadine wine, or blackberry wine." The fruit was harvested during the summer and early fall, mixed with sugar, then left in a crock to ferment until Thanksgiving, and some would be kept for years, Council recalled.

And then there is red drink. Today, Juneteenth tables and cookouts throughout the year feature brightly colored, sweet red drinks. This tradition may be the descendant of the African tradition of brewing a vividly colored beverage (variously called Red Sorrel, Sorrel, and Bissap) from kola nuts or roselle that has been carried on through generations of punch making, whether the red derives from cranberries, rhubarb, cherries, strawberries, or hibiscus flower petals, or even from the powdered drink mix Kool-Aid. The first published example of the African American practice of making and serving a sweet red-colored drink for summer appears in *The House Servant's Directory,* an 1827 recipe collection by Robert Roberts. His recipe "#55, To Make Raspberry, Strawberry, Cherry and All Kinds of Waters," used the heat of the sun to extract the juice from red fruit, which he mixed with water and sugar to create a "most delicious cool drink in hot weather."

Fruited or infused grain alcohol, such as liqueurs or cordials, expands upon this list of fermented sippables. Written recipes for steeping fruit with sugar and brandy until the flavors develop go back to 1866, when Malinda Russell, a free African American woman, featured recipes for blackberry, strawberry, and quince cordials in her collection, the *Domestic Cookbook*. Thirteen years later, a formerly enslaved woman, Abby Fisher, won a prize at the 1879 State Fair in Sacramento, California, for her Blackberry Brandy. And, more than a hundred years later, Edna Lewis kept this folk tradition alive, adding warm spices, black peppercorns, and bay leaf to the Blackberry Cordial in *The Gift of Southern Cooking: Recipes and Revelations from Two Great Southern Cooks.*

Sipped as is, or served chilled or over ice, ferments, cordials, and shrubs are experiencing a renaissance as a new generation of African American cookbook authors and barmasters reimagine the beverage-making ways of our ancestors.

BLACKBERRY BRANDY

To five gallons of berries add one gallon of the best brandy; put on fire in a porcelain kettle and let it just come to a boil, then take it off the fire and make a syrup of granulated sugar; ten pounds of sugar to one quart of water. Let the syrup cook till thick as honey, skimming off the foam while boiling; then pour it upon the brandy and berries and let it stand eight weeks; then put in bottle or demijohn. This blackberry brandy took a diploma at the State Fair [California] of 1879. Let the berries, brandy and syrup stand in a stone jar or bandy ket for eight weeks when you take it off the fire.

—Abby Fisher, *What Mrs. Fisher Knows About Old Southern Cooking,* 1881

STRAWBERRY WINE

Making homemade wine from deliciously sweet berries that grew on rambling wild bushes in the South is a throwback to the West African tradition of fermenting corn, sugarcane, and pineapple.

The process figured prominently in the charming cookbook Norma Jean Darden and her sister Carole wrote to preserve their family's culinary history, *Spoonbread and Strawberry Wine: Recipes and Reminiscences of a Family.*

Alongside memories of Papa Darden (their grandfather), who sold strawberry wine in his store from a spigoted barrel "at 10 cents a water glass," their cookbook provides a list of equipment and detailed tips for modern wine making, which begins with this wise counsel: "Wine making requires patience and a willingness to experiment. Try our method and use it to create your own."

This recipe is adapted from the Darden sisters' book. It is a perfect project to follow a trip to the pick-your-own berry farm. MAKES ABOUT 3 GALLONS

EQUIPMENT

Clean stoneware crock or plastic pail
(3- to 5-gallon capacity)

Cheesecloth

Funnel

4 to 6 one-gallon jugs with
fermentation locks

Siphon

12 one-quart mason jars or 16 wine bottles

WINE

7 pounds fresh-picked strawberries, hulled

2 gallons boiling water

Juice of 1 lemon

5 pounds granulated sugar

Mash the strawberries in the crock or pail. Add the boiling water, lemon juice, and sugar, and stir. Cover with cheesecloth and store at room temperature, 60 to 75 degrees, to ferment. Stir once daily to prevent mold from developing. Tiny bubbles will form around the edge of the mixture. Some cooks say the mixture will bubble and hiss. I didn't experience this, but it does give off a strong odor as the composition changes.

Strain the liquid into gallon jugs through a cheesecloth-lined funnel after 1 week, or "after the wine has quieted," as the old-timers used to say. (To make this task easier, you may want to first scoop out the fruit pulp with a strainer; just be sure to squeeze the pulp to release all the juice back into the crock, and then discard the pulp.) For best brewing, do not leave more than 2 inches of air space in the jugs. Lightly seal the jugs with

{recipe continues}

a fermentation lock. Do not disturb for at least 1 month, or until the wine is clear.

Use a siphon to remove the wine from one jug into a clean jug, leaving the sediment that has accumulated during fermentation in the bottom of the original jug. (Discard the sediment and clean the now-empty jug to use for the next jug. Or simply use clean new jugs for each jug. Pouring wine into a jug with the sediment can turn it to vinegar.) Separating the wine from the sediment is called "racking," and it's necessary to avoid a bitter taste and cloudy final product. Again seal the jugs with the fermentation locks. Rack again after two to four months if sediment returns. When the wine is clear and no longer bubbling, it is ready for bottling.

To bottle and cork the clear wine, siphon it into quart jars or wine bottles, leaving about 1 inch of air space at the top. Seal tightly. If using bottles with corks, place the bottles on their sides on a rack to keep the corks moist. Place the wine in a cool, dark place to age for 6 months to 2 years. The wine will mellow with age.

BLACKBERRY WINE

Have your berries gathered in the morning and pounded to a pulp. To every gallon of berries add 1 quart of boiling water. Strain. To every gallon of juice add 2 pounds white sugar. Fill a clean round cask, place it on its side on 2 pieces of scantling in your cellar, leaving the cask open for the wine to ferment and work over. Let stand 2 or 3 weeks, cork lightly, and leave it until December, a year is better.

—Emma Jane Jackson,
Emma Jane's Souvenir Cook Book, 1937

EMILY MEGGETT'S MUSCADINE WINE

Sweet, rich, and fruity, muscadine wine is the "unofficial official" holiday wine of the American South. It is everywhere in African American cookbooks, perhaps reflecting an ancestral memory that associates the fermented seasonal fruit with an African tradition—palm wine, and the medicinal use of muscadines to aid in digestion.

Palm wine, "known as 'African nectar' to early travelers, is drawn as sap from certain palm trees, bottled and kept for a few hours, or jounced about in a gourd on the back of a peddler, where it ferments and becomes quite intoxicating," as Ellen Gibson Wilson writes in her 1971 exploration of African foodways, *A West African Cook Book.* The wine may be poured on the ground as a gesture to the ancestors or offered on a visit to a family grave or funeral.

Many recipes for muscadine wine add a little active dry yeast to local grapes and sugar before setting it aside to ferment. Emily Meggett's does not. Known as the "Matriarch of Edisto Island," and, at 89 years old, the author of a *New York Times* bestselling 2022 debut cookbook, *Gullah Geechee Home Cooking*, she ferments the grapes and water for three months, then strains the juice, adds sugar, then lets it sit at least six months more before serving.

My heart was full the day Mrs. Meggett invited me into her kitchen, where she shared culinary wisdom while we cooked hoppin' John. As my film crew and I packed up our gear and prepared to leave, she gifted us each with a jar of plum wine, which she also keeps on hand for gifting.

I proudly share her recipe for muscadine wine without adaptation, and with gratitude. MAKES AT LEAST 10 SERVINGS

{recipe continues}

5 quarts muscadine (or other) grapes
5 pounds granulated sugar

Wash the grapes and put them in a 5-gallon water jug. The grapes should cover the bottom of the jug and reach the first ring. Fill the jug to the top ring with tepid water. Close the jug. In a few days, the grapes will start rising to the top. Let the grapes and water sit for 3 months. The grapes will burst open and eventually float to the top, and the wine will begin to change color.

Strain the juice into a bucket through a cheesecloth or a cloth pillowcase you don't mind staining. Be sure to squeeze the grapes to get all the juice out. Pull the pillowcase or cheesecloth from the bucket, rinse the pillowcase or cheesecloth, and strain again. Stir in the sugar and put the contents back into the jug. Let the wine sit for another 3 to 4 weeks. The longer it sits, the stronger it gets.

Strain again and, if needed, add more sugar to taste. Pour the wine into clean quart or pint glass jars, cover, and store in a cool place. (The wine will keep for about 6 months.)

COFFEE LIQUEUR

Coffee liqueur is a holiday tradition in my home, and not just served chilled with vodka and cream in a White Russian cocktail. The luscious Mexican-styled beverage Kahlúa, or its Jamaican counterpart Tia Maria, have been the basis for the cinnamon sticky buns I have baked to share with family and close friends on Christmas morning for more than forty years. Making the liqueur from scratch takes the meaning of hospitality to an entirely different level. The recipes for this are often found in African American cookbooks published after the 1980s, perhaps a response to popular advertising at the time that featured attractive couples enjoying the spirit.

Jessica B. Harris's recipe for Licor de Cafe in *The Africa Cookbook: Tastes of a Continent* is a sweet cordial made in the Cape Verde Islands with rum-infused, roasted coffee beans for a drink that smacks of molasses. Other formulas rely upon vodka, a neutral-tasting spirit, for steeping the vanilla and espresso beans. The process takes weeks, whichever spirit you choose.

I wanted a dazzling liqueur, and I wanted it to mature faster. Formulas made with instant coffee, which appeared in at least three cookbooks, put the product in the bottle sooner, but when I tested the recipes, the coffee flavor was muted. Strong brewed espresso simmered with rich-tasting demerara sugar created a cordial that was rich in earthy notes of chocolate and honey. I also took Harris's advice, sourcing Cachaça, the aged Brazilian spirit distilled from sugarcane juice, for my spirit, which gives the liqueur a mysterious quality and is worth trying. Vodka and Everclear grain alcohol were too harsh for my taste but may work for you. Ultimately, I like best the rum base.

The result here is a smooth liqueur that makes phenomenal coffee cocktails, or to take advice from Daisy Redman, one of the Savannah, Georgia, caterers featured in the 1980 cookbook *Four Great Southern Cooks*, it's wonderful over ice cream, fruit, or puddings. MAKES ABOUT 1 PINT

¾ cup strong hot espresso

1½ cups demerara sugar

¼ vanilla bean

6 ounces (¾ cup) rum, Cachaça, grain alcohol, or vodka

In a small saucepan over low heat, stir together the espresso, sugar, and vanilla bean with a wooden spoon until the sugar begins to dissolve. Increase the heat to medium and cook, stirring, until syrupy, 2 to 3 minutes.

Remove the pan from the heat and cool completely. Use a slotted spoon to remove the vanilla bean and discard.

Stir in the alcohol. Pour the mixture into a pint glass jar with a tight-fitting lid. Let stand at least 2 weeks before serving to allow the flavors to meld and mellow, shaking the jar occasionally.

HOME MADE KALUAH

Kaluah can be pretty costly, unless you get it duty-free in Mexico. We beat the system by making our own.

4 c. sugar

2 c. water

4 oz. Nescafé Instant coffee (others may do, but we found this the best)

1 whole vanilla bean

2 c. cheap vodka (it's the alcohol that's needed, so quality doesn't count)

Bring the water and sugar to a boil and add the instant coffee. Let stand for about 5 minutes, and add the cut open and quartered vanilla bean. When contents have cooled, add the vodka. Let it age at least 30 minutes before drinking. Don't try this recipe at a high altitude! You'll die of thirst waiting for it to come to a boil!

—Los Angeles Chapter,
South Central District Red Cross,
Favorite Recipes for Everyone, 1981

CRÈME DE MENTHE
Mint Cordial

Mention mint and alcohol in the same breath, and the Kentucky Derby's Mint Juleps most often come to mind. But the peppermint-flavored liqueur crème de menthe is also a popular and refreshing drink, served at room temperature or shaken with crushed ice until cold (about 10 seconds) to smooth out its syrupy nature. It's old school, a throwback to when sweet liqueurs were more popular, but it's not hard to find a love for that taste again, especially when you make it at home for a fresh flavor. (And if you do, a splash of this is a perfect stand-in for fresh mint in any of the recipes in this book where fresh mint is called for.)

You can also shake equal parts crème de menthe with Baileys Irish Cream, white crème de cacao, or Frangelico; top with a dollop of sweetened whipped cream; and drizzle with more green crème de menthe for a beautiful dessert cocktail.

In her 2014 book *Brown Sugar Kitchen: New-Style, Down-Home Recipes from Sweet West Oakland*, chef Tanya Holland substitutes brown sugar for granulated when making the simple syrup, and she tosses in the leaves from a whole bunch of mint to "bring a little California" to the Southern classic, Mint Julep. The brown sugar gives a complexity and the fresh mint an herbaceous, green note, with a more muted mint bite.

I like to make this cordial with young peppermint from my garden or when voluptuous bundles are on sale at the farmer's market. A double-steep of the herb, first with alcohol and then with syrup, layers the mint flavor. The simplified version that follows also includes an option with peppermint extract for its flavor. Even that tastes much better than the commercial stuff. MAKES ¾ PINT

⅔ cup lightly packed fresh peppermint leaves, torn into quarters (or 1 teaspoon peppermint extract; see Note)

2 ounces (¼ cup) Everclear Grain Alcohol

½ cup Simple Syrup (page 31)

½ teaspoon green food coloring (optional)

Place ⅓ cup of the mint leaves in a small jar with a tight-fitting lid. Pour in the Everclear and shake several times to mix. Cover and let stand 12 hours.

Strain and discard the mint, reserving the infused alcohol. Add the alcohol and simple syrup to a clean pint jar with a tight-fitting lid. Add the remaining ⅓ cup mint leaves, cover, and let stand 12 hours.

Strain and discard the mint. Stir in the food coloring, if desired, then cover and store for up to 30 days.

NOTE: To prepare with the mint extract, combine the extract, Everclear, and simple syrup in a pint jar with a tight-fitting lid. Close the lid and shake to mix well. Store for 2 to 3 weeks to allow the flavors to develop.

SIMPLE SYRUP

MAKES ABOUT 2 CUPS

2 cups granulated sugar

2 cups water

In a medium saucepan, combine the sugar and water, stirring until the sugar starts to dissolve. Bring to a boil over medium-high heat, then boil for 5 minutes, until syrupy. Remove from the heat and let cool completely. Store in the refrigerator, tightly covered, for up to 1 month.

MINT CORDIAL

For after-the-ball Carnival supper parties or receptions, brandied cherries and mint cordial are traditional—you may serve them separately, or, as most families in the Mardi Gras city do, combine them.

Obtain tender sprouts of fresh, crisp, young mint kissed only by the full-blown spring or early summer suns. A good handful of these mint sprigs—stems, leaves, and all—should be carefully washed. Shake the washed sprigs clear of water; lay them tenderly in a deep vessel, cover with good whiskey or brandy (bourbon), close the jar, and let stand 24 hours. Then strain through a coarse cloth, and to every quart of the liquor add 1 pint sugar. Stir well until all is dissolved, then bottle.

—Edith and John Watts, *Jesse's Book of Creole & Deep South Recipes, 1954*

MUSCADINE WINE
page 25

RASPBERRY SHRUB
page 36

SORREL
page 34

COFFEE LIQUEUR
page 28

**ERINE
EUR**
37

GINGER BEER
page 41

STRAWBERRY WINE
page 23

MINT CORDIAL
page 30

SORREL

Sorrel is a red flowering plant that blooms around Christmastime and is the basis for a traditional holiday beverage in the Caribbean, particularly Jamaica. The flowers are steeped with ginger, citrus juice, and spices to make a dark red aromatic drink that goes by the same name in the Caribbean. The beverage is called *jamaica* in Spanish-speaking cultures, and in Africa, "Nigerians call it *zobo*. Ghanaians call it *sobolo*, while Senegalese, Congolese, Malians, and Burkinabes call it *bissap*," as Marcus Samuelsson explains in his 2020 book, *The Rise: Black Cooks and the Soul of American Food.*

The following recipe is adapted from one in my 2019 cookbook, *Jubilee: Recipes from Two Centuries of African American Cooking.* It blends ingredients and techniques I learned from several cookbooks. Here are a few of those ideas:

First, you can personalize the spices according to your own tastes, substituting cardamom, nutmeg, or star anise for the cinnamon or cloves, and use up to ⅓ cup sliced fresh ginger, as is customary at Christmastime. And if you can't find fresh sorrel flowers, dried hibiscus flowers are a good substitute.

Additionally, the serving ideas for this drink are endless. Serve the sweet-tart beverage as is, dilute with sparkling water, or treat guests at your Juneteenth picnic to Hibiscus Tea Cocktails (see variation, page 35) by infusing the base with a splash of rum—dark, full-bodied Jamaican or light and dry white. I also love food writer Nicole Taylor's take in her 2022 Black celebrations cookbook, *Watermelon and Red Birds.* She pours the drink over a mound of crushed ice for a refreshing hot-weather treat: sorrel snow cones. And Marcus Samuelsson recommends ginger and hibiscus flower granita for a refreshing after-dinner palate cleanser in his 2020 book, *The Rise: Black Cooks and the Soul of American Food.* To make this drink into a granita, simply freeze it into a block, then scrape and scoop the crystals into chilled glasses.

Here's another fun fact from Enid Donaldson's 2000 book, *The Real Taste of Jamaica:* If you want to ferment the flowers the island way, cover the petals with boiling water and steep at room temperature for 24 hours, Add 1 tablespoon of uncooked rice to speed the process. MAKES 8 SERVINGS

6 cups water

2 cups fresh sorrel flowers or dried hibiscus flowers

2 tablespoons sliced peeled ginger, cut ¼ inch thick

1 (2- to 3-inch) cinnamon stick

6 whole cloves

¼ cup grated fresh orange zest

Grated zest and juice of 1 lemon or lime

½ cup cane syrup, honey, or agave nectar, or to taste

Mint leaves

8 lemon slices

In a large saucepan over medium heat, bring the water, flowers, ginger, cinnamon, cloves, and orange and lemon zests to a boil. Boil for 15 minutes. Remove the pot from the heat and stir in the lemon juice. Transfer to a bowl, cover, and refrigerate for 1 to 2 days to allow the flavors to mellow.

Strain and discard the solids. Stir in the syrup and serve, garnished with mint leaves and lemon slices.

VARIATION: For Hibiscus Tea Cocktails, stir ½ cup dark or white rum into the drink along with the desired sweetener. Fill Collins glasses one-half to two-thirds full with ice cubes. Pour in about 5 ounces (10 tablespoons) of hibiscus cocktail mix. Garnish with mint leaves and lemon slices.

RASPBERRY SHRUB

Back in colonial times, shrubs were fruit-infused vinegars created to preserve summer flavors, and were classically made from cherries, raspberries, blackberries, or currants. They were also popular cocktail mixers, often shaken with a clear spirit, sparkling water, or simply enjoyed diluted over ice cubes.

Old-time recipes for shrubs call for cooking a mixture of fruit and sugar to create a sweet juice, then mixing that with vinegar before storing. You can experiment with different types of vinegar and fruit combinations. When my fig tree is blooming, I make shrub with its purple globes. I have also taken shrub-making cues from recipe books, including those by early twentieth-century Pullman train chef Rufus Estes, early culinary researcher Thomas Bivins, and midcentury caterer Jessie Hargrave Payne, who added wild berries, currants, or cherries to the pot. And for an added twist, the contemporary Haitian American chef Gregory Gourdet relies upon coconut vinegar in his James Beard Award–winning 2021 cookbook, *Everyone's Table: Global Recipes for Modern Health.*

To help you determine your own favorite flavor combination, I suggest you start with this simple berry shrub, then try other fruits to make it your own. (Also try a splash in the Mint Julep recipe on page 183.) The yield varies depending upon how much liquid you extract from the fruit. MAKES 1½ TO 2 PINTS

---

2 cups fresh raspberries

2 cups granulated sugar

2 cups cider vinegar

In a medium bowl, combine the raspberries and sugar, and mash gently with a wooden spoon. Cover and refrigerate for 2 days, or until the sugar is dissolved and syrupy, stirring occasionally. Stir in the vinegar and return the bowl to the refrigerator for 2 more days.

Strain out the fruit pulp through a fine-mesh sieve, discarding it. Pour the liquid into a clean bottle or jar and seal with a tight-fitting lid. Refrigerate at least 1 week to allow the flavors to blend. (May be refrigerated up to 3 months.)

CURRANT SHRUB

Pick over and mash two quarts of ripe currants, add one pint of vinegar, and let stand over night. Set on the range and bring to the boiling point, then strain twice. Measure the clear liquid, and allow one cup of sugar to each cup of liquid. Simmer twenty minutes and seal in bottles.

—Rufus Estes, *Good Things to Eat as Suggested by Rufus,* 1911

TANGERINE LIQUEUR

Orange liqueur is a common mixer in classic cocktails like the Sidecar, and if you have lived long enough, drinks flavored with orange liqueur, such as the Beachcomber, the Blue Hawaii, or the Tequila Sunrise, bring you straight to the bright sandy beaches of the tropics.

But when you go to the liquor store and face a dozen or more bottles labeled "orange liqueur," there are a few things to consider.

First, that lone bottle of dry Curaçao is not the same as generic orange liqueurs, Cointreau, or Grand Marnier. It is a sweet and clear pot-stilled brandy flavored with the dried peels of a small, orange-like fruit grown on the Caribbean island of Curaçao. It comes in a variety of colors—red, green, amber, and blue.

Next, there is triple sec, which was originally made with less sugar than Curaçao, hence its name, *sec* meaning "dry" in French. Ask for triple sec at the liquor store, and the spirits manager is likely to steer you to Cointreau, a triple sec with subtle orange flavor and warm spices. It makes excellent cocktails.

Finally, the pricey squat bottle with the long neck is Grand Marnier, an orange liqueur in the Curaçao tradition. It is a blend of cognac and triple sec, and is laced with a hint of spice; it makes a delicious after-dinner digestif. I wouldn't mix with it.

I recommend buying sample sizes of several styles at various price points, including the luxurious French versions, as you develop your orange liqueur palate. Or, to simplify things, you can make your own liqueur with the following adaptation of a Jamaican recipe for a tangerine liqueur by cookbook author Enid Donaldson in *The Real Taste of Jamaica*. (Wine made from tangerine or ortanique juice, which is a cross between an orange and a tangerine, is also among her specialties.) The fragrance alone will awaken your senses and stir your imagination. And here I offer several spirit options so you can decide which flavor best suits your tastebuds—gin for its juniper notes, brandy with its extra sweetness, or woody rum. Before long, you will mix Cosmopolitans like a pro. MAKES ABOUT 1 QUART

{recipe continues}

10 tangerines or clementines

24 ounces (3 cups) gin; or 12 ounces
(1½ cups) brandy; or 16 ounces
(2 cups) rum

2 cups Simple Syrup (page 31)

Wash and peel the tangerines or clementines.
Cut the peel into ⅛-inch-thick strips.
(Reserve the fruit for another use.) Place the
skins and gin in a 1-quart glass jar with a
tight-fitting lid. Cover and let stand 24 to
48 hours, until the flavor develops, shaking
occasionally.

   Strain and discard the peels, reserving the
infused gin. Wash the jar and set aside to
reuse. Combine the syrup and flavored gin
in the clean jar. Cover and store for 30 days
before serving.

CURACAO

*Into a bottle which will hold a full quart,
or a little over, drop 6 ounces of Orange
Peel sliced very thin, and add 1 pint of
Whiskey. Cork the bottle securely and
let it stand two weeks, shaking the bottle
frequently during that time. Next strain
the mixture, add the Syrup, pour the
strained mixture back into the cleaned
bottle and let it stand 3 days, shaking
well now and then during the first day.
Next, pour a teacupful of the mixture into
a mortar and beat up with it 1 drachm
Powdered Alum, 1 drachm Carbonate of
Potash. Put this mixture back into the
bottle and let it stand for 10 days, at the
expiration of which time the Curacao will
be clear and ready for use.*

—Tom Bullock, *The Ideal Bartender*, 1917

TANGERINE LIQUEUR

GINGER BEER

Making ginger beer is an African custom that is seemingly as old as time. I loved finding a step-by-step recipe aimed at next-generation cooks in Fran Osseo-Asare's 1993 exploration of West African foodways, *A Good Soup Attracts Chairs: A First African Cookbook for American Kids*. Osseo-Asare reminds us that making this "does take patience and planning, but it keeps well and can be made ahead for a party."

Some Diasporan formulas, including this recipe, are odes to the original that requires several days of natural fermentation for the ingredients to meld into an effervescent punch. Others take a shortcut by adding a bit of yeast to speed the process.

Having none of that, the provocateurs behind the artistic and revolutionary 2022 cookbook *Ghetto Gastro Presents Black Power Kitchen,* by Jon Gray, Pierre Serrao, and Lester Walker, known together as Ghetto Gastro, begin their recipe with a starter culture, or "bug"—something they learned from Jon's mother, Denise, who emphasized ginger's probiotic qualities. Their recipe, Ginger Me, combines fresh ginger, water, and sugar in a jar. The starter rests in a warm place for two to three days, and more of each ingredient is added throughout the process. When the bug becomes "vigorously bubbly," it's ready to mix with a tea that's been brewed from more ginger, sugar, water, and lemon, as the recipe explains.

This somewhat more streamlined version throws to Questlove's 2019 book, *Mixtape Potluck.* It's a recipe by way of Thelma Golden, director of the Studio Museum of Harlem. It is not fizzy like the Ghetto Gastro version. Nor does it bubble in the soda pop sense. It is tangy and, depending on the particulars of your environment, may or may not have a touch of alcohol in the final product. SERVES 4 TO 6

¾ cup peeled and coarsely chopped fresh ginger

½ cup granulated sugar

Grated zest and juice of 1 lime

2 cups boiling water

2 cups cold water

½ cup lemon juice

Ice cubes

In a jar or crock, combine the ginger, sugar, and lime zest and juice. Pour in the boiling water and stir to dissolve the sugar. Let stand 15 minutes. Stir in the cold water. Cover loosely with cheesecloth, place on the kitchen counter, and let rest at room temperature, away from sunlight, to ferment for 1 to 2 days, stirring daily, until the mixture has a pleasant tang. The mixture will not bubble.

Strain the mixture into a pitcher and add the lemon juice. Serve in glasses, poured over ice.

FONIO BEER

The beer-brewing tradition among African housewives is centuries old. Depending upon the region, the fermented beverage might be made from corn, grains, or even bananas. Ellen Gibson Wilson describes the homebrew this way in her 1971 book, *A West African Cook Book*: "West African beer is usually light brown, cloudy and somewhat bitter. During the hungry season, which strikes subsistence farmers in the last weeks before the new harvest, some householders turn most of their scanty hoards of grain into beer."

This recipe tweaks a formula in Pierre Thiam's 2019 collection, *The Fonio Cookbook: An Ancient Grain Rediscovered*, inspired by his aunt Estelle-Genevieve Soukpo Thiam, of Benin. Fonio is a gluten-free, nutrient-dense, ancient grain with a slightly nutty, earthy flavor. A member of the millet family, fonio is known among the Dogon People of Mali as "the Seed of the Universe—the grain at the root of all existence"—according to Thiam. Fonio is a reliable agricultural crop; it survives even with very little water or attention and is a good luck charm. While moms put some fonio in children's bags on the first day of school, you can serve this recipe for Fonio Beer to guests as a gesture of hospitality. MAKES ABOUT 2 QUARTS

---

4 cups raw fonio, rinsed and drained well

2 quarts distilled water

6 makrut lime leaves or zest and juice of 1 lime

1½ cups granulated sugar, plus more as needed

In a large glass bowl or other glass container, soak the fonio in the water for 1 to 2 days at room temperature, away from the sun and covered with a cheesecloth. When soaked thoroughly, the grains should feel pasty in your hands.

Working in batches, if necessary, put the fonio and water in a blender and blend well. Return it to the bowl and cover again with clean cheesecloth. Allow to ferment for 2 days, away from the sun. The mixture should have a strong but pleasant fermented flavor.

Line a fine-mesh sieve with cheesecloth and strain the liquid into a large pot. Add the lime and sugar, and bring to a boil over high heat. Reduce the heat to medium and boil for 1 hour, until fragrant. Adjust the flavor with more sugar, if you like. Strain the mixture through several layers of cheesecloth, then transfer to glass jars and refrigerate. Serve chilled.

GRAIN BEER IS MADE THIS WAY

The grain is soaked or dampened and allowed to sprout. Then it is dried and ground. This ground meal is boiled with water for a considerable period. It is then strained and allowed to stand and ferment overnight, or longer. It is boiled again, and, when cooled, is ready to drink.

—Ellen Gibson Wilson, *A West African Cook Book*, 1971

BERRY LIQUEUR

Klancy Miller, cookbook author and publisher of *For the Culture*, a magazine high-lighting Black women and femmes in food, and I agree that concocting liqueurs at home is a great do-it-yourself project. Here, she relies upon strawberries, the spring-time favorite, but home cooks recorded recipes for cordials made with wild fruit, such as blackberries, raspberries, and cherries, as far back as the nineteenth century. The spirit is perfect on its own over ice or mixed into a summertime cocktail combining Champagne, prosecco, or white wine with orange liqueur, and garnishing with mint. MAKES 1 PINT

3 cups fresh strawberries or blackberries
16 ounces (2 cups) vodka or brandy
⅓ cup granulated sugar

Hull and quarter the strawberries; alternatively, you may keep them whole, which makes for a pretty bottle until the berries wilt. In a clean 1-quart mason jar or other lidded glass container, combine the berries, vodka, and sugar. Close the lid tightly and shake well to dissolve the sugar. Store the jar in the refrigerator for 1 month, shaking it every few days.

Use a slotted spoon to remove the berries. Then cover again and store in the refrigerator. (The liqueur will keep for up to 3 months.)

CORDIAL

Select and prepare berries as if to make jelly; use no water. To each pint of juice add one pound of sugar. To a pint use one teaspoon of ground cinnamon, one-fourth teaspoon of ground mace, one teaspoon of ground cloves. Boil in the liquid 30 minutes, strain, add a glass of best brandy; bottle. This is excellent for babies with summer complaint, and is fine for diarrhoea.

—Atholene Peyton, *The Peytonia Cook Book*, 1906

2

BATCH

Caterers

CATERERS

*The fiddlers in the balcony doubtless gave the touch that only
music can supply to any gay assemblage. Fires were burning
brightly on the hearths "and all went merry as a marriage bell."
As the evening wore on the gay ladies were escorted to the supper
room, where the caterer had prepared his most famous dishes
and brought forth his finest wines.*

—Hamilton Hall Cookbook, *1947*

I paid just $11 for a 1947 edition of the *Hamilton Hall Cookbook*. It's an unusual entry in my library because the book of recipes was not authored by a person of color, nor is it rare, but the spiral-bound collection is nevertheless a treasure chest. It contains biographical sketches of two well-respected caterers managing food service at Hamilton Hall—John Remond and Edward P. Cassell—and these profiles put flesh on the bones of what little is known about African American caterers and food enterprise operators serving spirits in early America—whether they were enslaved or newly freed.

Hamilton Hall was a beautiful gathering place, built in 1805 in Salem, Massachusetts. It was renowned for its elite social gatherings and sophisticated dinners served by candlelight. John Remond, a native of the Caribbean island of Curaçao and a free man of color, rose to prominence as the "Colored Restaurateur" of Hamilton Hall.

A paper presented to the American Antiquarian Society in 1985, entitled *The Remonds of Salem, Massachusetts: A Nineteenth-Century Family Revisited*, explains that Remond lived in one of Hamilton Hall's apartments for fifty years, during which time he maintained a gourmet shop on its first floor. Media and socialites' reports described him as an "aristocrat of his profession," a man of "unceasing personal industry and shrewd business acumen."

In 1808, he began collecting rare and fine wines from faraway lands such as Portugal and Bordeaux, which he sold with other luxuries of the era. One year later, the list of goods he advertised for sale shows his dexterity as a proficient event planner and a thriving trader: 10,000 pounds of Virginia and Carolina hams; 2,000 pounds of pork shoulders; 4,000 pounds of Albany-cured smoked beef; 3,000 pounds of new milk cheese; 300 dozen of Newark and crabapple cider; 300 glass pots of pickled oysters; 100 glass pots of pickled lobsters; 300 gallons of wine vinegar; and New York ale. Spanish cigars, madeira, sherry, claret barrels of whiskey, spices, macaroni, and exquisite desserts were also stocked in his store.

In addition to selling luxury items, Remond and his wife, Nancy, an accomplished cake baker and cook, earned reputations for the delicious fare they prepared in a Rumford kitchen—a space centered around a state-of-the-art fireplace, known variously as the Rumford oven, the Rumford fireplace, or the Rumford Roaster. Their dazzling feasts included, according to hamiltonhall.org, such delicacies as turtle soup, beef à la mode, baked codfish, oyster pies, roasted pigs, Bremen geese, woodcocks, plovers, pigeons, quails, partridges, baked calf heads, and lobster. The Governor of Massachusetts, the Marquis de Lafayette, and Nathaniel Bowditch all dined at their table, and the "oven" is still displayed at Hamilton Hall today.

And there's another thing to know about the Remonds. Beyond the fancy dinners for pedigreed guests and the inventory of fine foods, the couple inspired their children to carry on their catering legacy and to do so as activists fighting for important causes like the antislavery movement or women's rights movement.

Townsfolk couldn't get enough of daughter Susan's pastries, jellies, confections, and fancy desserts. They were also intrigued by her activists' kitchen. Throughout the mid-1820s, Susan maintained a small, popular dining room where exquisite food and a variety of fine wines, liquors, and cordials were served to an exclusive clientele. The American Antiquarian Society paper notes that her kitchen was a "'mecca' where gathered radicals, free thinkers, abolitionists, female suffragists, fugitives and others who found rest and refreshment for mind and body."

Hamilton Hall maintained its reputation for excellent food and beverage service long after the memory of the Remonds faded, thanks to its next-generation caterer, Edward P. Cassell.

A biographical sketch in my disintegrating, 75-year-old copy of the *Hamilton Hall Cookbook* depicts "dignified Edward P. Cassell . . . delivering a coveted invitation to an Assembly, a debutante ball or a wedding at which he was to be major-domo of

These profiles put flesh on the bones of what little is known about African American caterers and food enterprise operators serving spirits in early America—whether they were enslaved or newly freed.

the supper room. He was an artist in creating both fine effects and fine suppers . . . the ice-cream cat with a blue ribbon and bell around its neck, the ice-cream hen and chickens in a nest of spun sugar, the great platters of salmon and meats, the game, and the bowls of chicken, lobster and salmon salads all stir nostalgic memories." Beverage recipes in *Hamilton Hall Cookbook* run the gamut—from fermented elderberry wine to, befitting the craft of the caterer, bewitching drinks mixed for a crowd, such as tea punch, egg nog, and claret cup.

Interestingly, the recipe for Hamilton Hall's distinctive rum punch is not included in the book. Nor is it mentioned in a *Boston Globe* book review dated June 22, 1947, even though several online sources today center Cassell's reputation on his "perfected rum punch recipe."

With no explanation for the missing link between Cassell and the recipe, I did a little more digging through my cookbook collection to see if there were any Black authors who had embraced rum punch, a drink notoriously connected to the Middle Passage, sugar plantations, and rum makers. I located a strikingly similar formula in Massachusetts in the 1827 house servants' manual published by the Governor's Mansion butler, Robert Roberts, and another one, printed nearly a century later in a compilation of domestic-science-focused recipes, *The Peytonia Cook Book,* by Atholene Peyton.

Roberts's recipe "#79—To Make a Beautiful Flavoured Punch" calls for lemon, sugar, Jamaican rum, and brandy, a combination resembling British Aarack Punch. Peyton refines the instructions. She laces a "strong, sweet lemonade" with rum and brandy, helping audiences see the adaptability of spiked citrus ade.

Both formulas are a long distance from the syrupy-sweet, tropical rum punches of today. And both reminded me that social history and the life stories recorded in Black cookbooks together transform hospitality workers' reputations from mindless servants to intelligent entrepreneurs. That makes me proud.

CHAMPAGNE PUNCH

CHAMPAGNE PUNCH

The beautiful Champagne Cocktail that appears in my cookbook, *Jubilee: Recipes from Two Centuries of African American Cooking*, is an adaptation that slims down Tom Bullock's fruit-based punch bowl, a beverage that boasts a fat spirits list (see his original recipe, opposite).

Atholene Peyton's recipe from *The Peytonia Cook Book*, published in 1906, takes us back to the punch bowl, with her simple mix of homemade lemonade concentrate sweetened with a luscious fruit syrup that is then spiked with a bright Champagne. For a festive beverage with lots of bubbles, sparkling water and/or ginger ale may be added. And for a heady drink with all the flourishes a barmaster can imagine, you can stir in a bit of brandy and rum, as well as sparkling water (which helps balance the spirits), as Julian Anderson did in his 1919 collection, *Julian's Recipes*. Or top off the punch with the flavorful liqueur Curaçao and a dash of Peychaud's bitters à la the great Creole chef Lena Richard. Fresh raspberries and raspberry syrup are also nice additions.

My recipe leans into the more streamlined mimosa-styled cocktails recommended in cookbooks by Black caterers Rebecca West and Bessie Munson, here relying on citrus, fresh pineapple, and strawberry syrup or maraschino cherry juice to flavor the Champagne. SERVES 6

---

1 cup granulated sugar

Grated zest and juice of 1 lemon

¼ cup strawberry syrup or maraschino cherry juice

1 (750 ml) bottle Champagne

1 block of ice

1 orange, sliced

3 slices fresh pineapple

Combine the sugar, lemon zest and juice, and syrup in a pint jar. Stir to mix well, then cover and refrigerate for 2 hours, or until completely chilled.

Pour the lemon-sugar mixture into a punch bowl. Gradually add the Champagne and ice, stirring gently to mix. Float the orange and pineapple slices on top of the punch to garnish. When serving, ladle the punch into Champagne flutes.

CHAMPAGNE CUP

For mixing use a large Punch bowl or other suitable vessel of glass or porcelain lined.

4 oranges sliced

4 lemons sliced

½ pineapple, sliced

½ pint Chartreuse

½ pint Abricontine

1 pint Curaçao

1 pint Cognac Brandy

1 pint Tokay wine

Stir well and allow mixture to stand three hours. Strain into another bowl and add:

3 quarts Champagne

3 pints Apollinaris Water

1 large piece ice

Stir well; decorate with Fruit; float slices of Grape Fruit on top and serve in Champagne Glasses.

—Tom Bullock, *The Ideal Bartender*, 1917

JERK-SPICED
BLOODY MARY
page 56

JERK-SPICED BLOODY MARY

The Bloody Mary has long been a popular morning-after drink, known for its ability to soothe symptoms of a hangover. There are just a few recipes in my collection of African American cookbooks for the classic combination, which is ordinarily made with vodka, tomato juice, Worcestershire sauce, and seasonings, but the drink is experiencing a bit of a renaissance lately. The Bottomless Bloody Mary on restaurant brunch menus, made more boldly with rum, flavored vodka, and potent spices, may be driving this trend.

I love the flavor departure in the Bloody Maria, a fiery Mexican version built with tequila; or the complexity of iconic restaurateur-model-author-entrepreneur Barbara "B." Smith's Cajun Mary, which she included in *B. Smith Cooks Southern-Style* in 2009. Smith's ode to Louisiana can be made sweet with Absolut Mango vodka or spicy with Absolut Pepper vodka and garnished with spicy baby okra and blue cheese–stuffed olives. And my curiosity was definitely piqued by Pat and Gina Neely's flavor-balancing act. The television food personalities reimagined the morning libation with hot-pepper vodka, vegetable juice, barbecue sauce, and horseradish in their 2009 cookbook, *Down Home with the Neelys: A Southern Family Cookbook.*

I also fell hard for the idea of Bloody Marys for a Crowd, in Elle Simone Scott's 2022 cookbook, *Boards*—so hard that I included a version of the recipe in *Cook's Country* magazine, where I am editor-in-chief. Elle starts by making a big batch of classic Bloodies, but for variety, she sets out a wide assortment of rim salts, skewers, and garnishes—everything from classic olives and celery to chicken wings and poached shrimp—so people can customize their drink to their heart's content.

In the end, though, it was the Bloody Mary à la Jerk, included in Helen Willinsky's 1990 book, *Jerk Barbecue from Jamaica,* that won me over. Inspired by its use of sweet-hot spices, the version that follows swaps rum for vodka and doubles easily to serve a large crowd. Rimming the outside edge of the serving glass with the jerk seasoning intensifies the island experience, but it is optional. SERVES 8 TO 10

1 quart tomato juice or Campbell's V8 juice

½ cup plus 1 tablespoon prepared jerk seasoning

1 teaspoon celery salt

1½ tablespoons Worcestershire sauce

½ cup fresh lime or lemon juice

½ to 1½ teaspoons hot pepper sauce, or to taste

1 cup light or dark rum

Ice cubes

8 to 10 lime or lemon wedges

8 to 10 celery stalks, with leaves

Combine the tomato juice, 1 tablespoon of the jerk seasoning, the celery salt, and Worcestershire sauce in a small microwave-safe pitcher. Microwave until bubbles just begin to form around the edge of the pitcher, 2 to 3 minutes. Remove it from the microwave and stir to dissolve the seasoning. Add the lime juice, hot pepper sauce, and rum to the base. Refrigerate several hours, until thoroughly chilled.

Place the remaining ½ cup jerk seasoning on a saucer. Moisten the edges of tall glasses with a lime wedge. Press the edge of each glass into the seasoning to create a spiced rim. Add ice to each glass, then pour in the mix. Garnish each glass with 1 lime wedge and a celery stalk.

CLARET CUP

Cups are wine-forward drinks decorated with fruit and herbs. Classic cups can have a base of either wine or beer. For the wine-based, claret (a red wine) and lemonade form the foundation, with brandy, green Chartreuse or Curaçao, and pineapple or cherry juice stirred into the more elaborate mixes. Despite the name, cups are served from pitchers or other large vessels, similar to punch. Cucumber was a popular adornment that is back on craft-cocktail menus.

Bertha L. Turner, a state superintendent of domestic science who, in 1910, cultivated recipes from members of the Colored Women of the State of California for *The Federation Cook Book*, fortifies her Old Pacific Slope Punch with twice the claret I suggest in my adaptation that follows. Despite its fruity foundation, this cocktail is not as sweet as the version in John B. Goins's 1914 book, *The American Waiter*. (Goins was an expert in early twentieth-century lodging and hospitality, not a recipe specialist.) And the addition of seasonal grapefruit is a nice touch that delivers potent citrus notes without dominating the wine and Champagne flavors.

The word *claret* is derived from the Latin meaning "clear." It is a British term used to group the red-wine blends of Bordeaux into one category, which gives you lots of flexibility when it comes to choosing the wine for this recipe. Try making it with your favorite Cabernet Sauvignon or Merlot. Served in small tea cups, this cocktail is good as a prelude to Thanksgiving dinner. SERVES 30

1 tablespoon granulated sugar

2 tablespoons warm water

3 oranges, sliced

2 lemons, sliced

1 pineapple, peeled, cored, and sliced into rings

1 ounce (2 tablespoons) Abricotine or apricot brandy

2 ounces (¼ cup) Curaçao or ¼ cup homemade Tangerine Liqueur (page 37)

2 (750 ml) bottles claret of choice

2 (750 ml) bottles Champagne or other sparkling white wine

2 cups sparkling water

1 large block of ice

1 grapefruit, thinly sliced and cut into half-moons

{recipe continues}

In a large bowl, stir together the sugar and warm water, stirring until the sugar is dissolved. Add the orange, lemon, and pineapple slices, and stir to thoroughly coat the fruit with the syrup. Let stand for 30 minutes, allowing the fruit to macerate.

Add the Abricotine, Curaçao, and claret, and stir for 1 minute. Cover and refrigerate for 3 hours.

Strain the mixture through a fine-mesh sieve, pressing on the pulp with a spoon to extract all the fruit juice. Pour the infused wine, Champagne, and sparkling water into a punch bowl. Stir gently to mix. Add the ice block and garnish with grapefruit slices. To serve, ladle the drink into Champagne flutes or punch cups.

CLARET PUNCH

3½ quarts best claret.

1 pint maraschino.

1½ pounds cut sugar.

Rind of one cucumber.

1 quart Apollinaris water.

Decorate with sliced oranges.

—John B. Goins, *The American Waiter,* 3rd edition, 1914

DAIQUIRIS FOR A PARTY

This Cuban cocktail of rum, lemon or lime juice, and sugar is a classic sour that is well known and popular today, but it was considered exotic in the early years of the twentieth century. It was so new at that time that barmaster Julian Anderson spelled its name phonetically to help his readers, calling it "Dai-qui-ri Cocktail" in the second-ever cocktail book by a Black man, *Julian's Recipes.*

Today, we think of the Daiquiri as a foundational cocktail. Muddle mint leaves into it and you have a Mojito. The Caipirinha is essentially a Daiquiri flavored with Cachaça, a fragrant Brazilian spirit distilled from sugarcane; it is Brazil's national drink.

Here, I sweeten this crowd-pleaser with lime-infused simple syrup for a balanced drink that is neither too sweet nor too sour. And while you should feel free to try it with any of the light Caribbean rums, do avoid the temptation to substitute lime-flavored alcohol. Fresh lime juice is an absolute must, and I include the aromatic zest as well.

I make the mix in batches, as Jeanne Louise Duzant Chance did in her 1985 cookbook, *Ma Chance's French Caribbean Creole Cooking.* I also love the cultural mash-up in *Between Harlem and Heaven: Afro-Asian-American Cooking for Big Nights, Weeknights, and Every Day,* a 2018 book by chefs JJ Johnson and Alexander Smalls. They brighten the drink with Thai makrut lime leaves, which can be found among the dried herbs in the Asian food aisle of some supermarkets or in the freezer section; the leaves also are easy to purchase online.

Another variation, the Frozen Daiquiri, which is mixed in a blender with extra ice, is a slushy chiller. Make it with frozen fruit—be it strawberry, banana, or mango—for a summertime treat. SERVES 4

{recipe continues}

½ cup fresh lime juice

¼ cup granulated sugar

Grated zest of 1 lime

12 ounces (1½ cups) white rum

4 cups crushed ice (see page 184)

Slices or twists of lime

In a small saucepan over low heat, combine the lime juice and sugar, stirring to dissolve, for 2 to 3 minutes. Remove from the heat, add the lime zest, and cool to room temperature. Strain the lime syrup through a fine-mesh strainer into a medium bowl. Add the rum and stir to mix well. Cover and refrigerate until thoroughly chilled.

Distribute the crushed ice among four rocks glasses. Stir the Daiquiri mixture, then pour into the glasses over the ice. Garnish each with a lime wheel or twist.

VARIATION: To make Frozen Daiquiris, combine the chilled Daiquiri mixture in a blender with 1½ cups ice and 1 cup chunks of frozen fresh fruit (½ cup chopped mango, crushed pineapple, or sliced strawberries; ½ medium pitted peach, or a small banana), and 1 ounce (2 tablespoons) fruit liqueur as desired. (Tempus Fugit Crème de Banane makes exceptional Banana Daiquiris.) Blend on high speed until the mixture is thick and slushy. Serve in cocktail glasses along with a short straw.

DAIQUIRIS FOR A PARTY

SPICED WINE

Spiced or mulled wine is an ideal beverage to serve guests on a chilly winter evening. Black cookbook authors have long simmered red wine, brandy, cinnamon, cloves, and cardamom with winter citrus fruits for a warm expression of hospitality. In the early twentieth century, mixologist Tom Bullock simplified the concept, serving a cocktail of port, ginger, and brandy topped with a dusting of nutmeg.

In 1983, a recipe for Glogg, a spiced Swedish drink served garnished with raisins and blanched almonds, appeared in *Forty Years in the Kitchen* by Dorothy Shanklin Russey, alongside the caterer's kitchen notes and recipes for fine cooking.

The timeless tradition is reimagined again in this cultural mashup inspired by the spiced wine in Jennifer Booker's *Field Peas to Foie Gras* and Ponche Navideño (Mexican Christmas Fruit Punch), a popular drink that is fragrant with tamarind, guava, and piloncillo, a type of raw cane sugar shaped like a cone. To make it your own, choose a full-bodied Spanish tempranillo or a French burgundy. Try different herb and spice blends to add interest, such as ginger, allspice, peppercorns, rosemary, or thyme. Toss in a few dried hibiscus flowers for a tart surprise. And serve garnished with a few whole spices or fruits to add personality—whole cranberries, star anise, sliced oranges, and black peppercorns. SERVES 6

Peels of 2 oranges

Peel of 1 lemon

10 to 12 dried hibiscus flowers

2 or 3 cardamom pods

2 or 3 star anise pods

3 or 4 cloves

8 cinnamon sticks

1 bottle (750 ml) dry Spanish red wine or French burgundy

1 cup cognac or brandy

¼ cup brown sugar

1 or 2 oranges, sliced, for garnish

Trim and discard the white pith from the orange and lemon peels. Place the peels, hibiscus flowers, cardamom pods, star anise, cloves, and 2 cinnamon sticks in a piece of cheesecloth and tie with string to enclose the aromatics.

Add this spice sachet, the red wine, brandy, and sugar to a large saucepan. Bring to simmer over low heat, stirring to dissolve the sugar. Simmer lightly—do not boil—for 10 minutes to allow the flavors to blend. Remove the sachet. Serve immediately in warmed, heatproof glasses garnished with orange wheels and the reserved cinnamon sticks. (Or, you may keep it warm on the stove over very low heat for up to 2 hours.)

ICED COFFEE PUNCH

Coffee and ice cream "cappuccino" is a festive party drink that shows up often as a hostess favorite in Black cookbooks; it allowed coffee aficionados to savor the beverage's nutty goodness even on hot summer afternoons.

In Carolyn Quick Tillery's 2006 cookbook, *Southern Homecoming Traditions,* pantry staples like chocolate syrup and amaretto liqueur turn strong brewed coffee into a deliciously rich and frosty drink. Meanwhile, over in Texas, caterer extraordinaire Bessie Munson's 1980 cookbook, *Bless the Cook,* features a recipe for Party Chocolate Cappuccino that is pure decadence, laced with white crème de menthe, brandy, chocolate mint liqueur, and billows of whipped cream.

Rose Elder, whose husband Lee was the first African American to play in the US Masters Golf Tournament at the Augusta National Golf Club in Georgia, sticks close to the simplicity of the original recipe (and many published versions) in her collection, *Golfers Cookbook.* Here, instant coffee is steeped and chilled, then cold milk and chocolate ice cream swirl together with a bit of almond flavoring or amaretto for a creamy concoction that reminds me of an uber-rich coffee-chocolate shake.

I snatched elements from all of these for my adaptation. I wanted the kind of frosty and luscious drink you might pick up in see-through plastic to-go cups, but with a little buzz. You can serve it for dessert. The choice of spirit is yours—brandy delivers the most potent flavor, while the subtle taste of vodka will almost disappear. And, feel free to make it with decaffeinated coffee and omit the spirit flourishes, if you like. SERVES 20

2 cups strong brewed coffee or espresso

2 tablespoons demerara sugar

1 ounce semi-sweet chocolate, chopped

1 quart cold whole milk

1 cup brandy, cognac, bourbon, or vodka

2 pints vanilla or chocolate ice cream, or 1 pint of each

Whipped cream

Chocolate syrup or liqueur (optional)

Chocolate shavings or cocoa nibs (optional)

Heat the coffee, sugar, and chopped chocolate in a medium saucepan over medium heat, stirring until the sugar is dissolved and the chocolate is melted. Remove it from the heat and allow it to cool to room temperature.

Pour the chocolate-coffee mixture into a large jar and refrigerate, covered, until cold, at least 4 hours. Stir in the milk and brandy. Chill thoroughly. Spoon chunks of ice cream into individual tumblers or mason jars. Pour about 1 cup spiked coffee over the ice cream, and garnish with whipped cream. If desired, add chocolate syrup and shavings on top.

PLANTER'S PUNCH

Sugar plantations throughout the Caribbean had their own recipes for Planter's Punch, the island drink that's served in large quantities or in individual portions. The opacity of the plantation system blurred my search for this drink's origin story, which is noticeably missing from scholarly writings and cookbooks alike.

It may be rooted in the plantation practice of incentivizing and rewarding enslaved workers (including the children) with strong liquor, sometimes mixed with water and sugar. One legend says that a Jamaican planter's wife made the combination to quench the thirsts of her laborers, though we can see today that would be at best a mixed blessing.

But also today, we can reclaim this recipe. Bar educator Tiffanie Barriere, who consulted with me on this book, created the punch bowl rendition here. It features more citrus and grenadine (homemade for more complexity) than are traditional, and the bitters often included in the mix are omitted for balance. This makes for a refreshing beverage that is bright, far less sweet, and festive enough for a crowd.

SERVES 14 TO 16

⅔ cup fresh lemon juice

⅔ cup fresh orange juice

¼ cup fresh lime juice

¾ cup Simple Syrup (page 31)

12 ounces (1½ cups) dark Jamaican rum

12 ounces (1½ cups) white rum

3 cups water

1 large block of ice

2 ounces (¼ cup) homemade Pomegranate Grenadine (page 73)

Lemon slices

Orange slices

To a punch bowl, add the lemon, orange, and lime juices and stir in the syrup. Stir in the rums and water. Gently lay in the block of ice and then pour the grenadine on top of the floating ice. Stir for 5 to 10 seconds, allowing the grenadine to turn the punch slightly pink. Garnish with lemon and orange wheels. Ladle into punch cups or pour over crushed ice in rocks glasses.

POMEGRANATE-DEMERARA RUM PUNCH

In *Jubilee: Recipes from Two Centuries of African American Cooking*, I share the mnemonic poem that helps barmasters remember how to make this Caribbean-style rum punch. The measures may be in cups or gallons, but the ratios must always be the same. They are:

1 part sour (fresh lime juice)
2 parts sweet (simple syrup and/or grenadine)
3 parts strong (rum)
4 parts weak (fruity juices)

Since then, I have upped my game for making these sweet, tropical cocktails taste even more refreshing by learning from new masters, like Shannon Mustipher, whose 2019 book, *Tiki: Modern Tropical Cocktails,* is a recent addition to my collection. This recipe for Pomegranate-Demerara Rum Punch takes its name from demerara rum, a spirit distilled in the English style in the Demerara River valley of Guyana. It is "especially prized for heady floral and concentrated berry notes, smoke, and a chewy texture—qualities imparted by rich alluvial soils," as Mustipher explains.

To make this punch top shelf, I have accented the rum's deep sugarcane notes with homemade orange and pineapple juices that I press myself in a masticating juicer. I also keep my Pomegranate Grenadine (recipe follows), the ubiquitous sweet-tart crimson syrup, in the fridge to give my cocktails a sweet red blush.

The Pomegranate Shine in Matthew Raiford's beautiful 2021 collection of Gullah Geechee recipes, *Bress 'n' Nyam,* inspired me to try my hand at homemade grenadine. Raiford macerates chunks of whole pomegranates and ginger in Everclear, a high-octane grain alcohol, for 45 days, then strains the juice into a simple syrup and ages the cordial an additional month and a half.

My interpretation of the grenadine that follows is a nonalcoholic pomegranate syrup, made by warming rich demerara sugar with pomegranate juice, and enriching it with a touch of orange and pomegranate molasses. This flavorful mixer stands in for store-bought grenadine in cocktails like Tequila Sunrise, Clover Club, the

{recipe continues}

Hurricane, and here in Rum Punch. Teetotalers will like the way this homemade grenadine brightens up sparkling soda or ginger ale when served over ice.

Serve this cocktail anytime, but especially as summer draws to a close on September 20th—National Rum Punch Day. SERVES 10

8 ounces (1 cup) Jamaican white rum

8 ounces (1 cup) dark Jamaican or demerara rum

8 ounces (1 cup) coconut rum

2½ cups fresh pineapple juice

2½ cups fresh orange juice

¼ cup fresh lime juice

1 cup water

1 large block of ice

⅓ cup Pomegranate Grenadine (recipe follows)

Orange slices

Pineapple wedges or leaves from the crown

In a punch bowl, combine the rums and fruit juices. Stir in the water and mix well. Cover and refrigerate at least 2 hours, until thoroughly chilled.

When ready to serve, add the block of ice to the punch bowl and stir 1 to 2 minutes to slightly dilute the punch. Ladle the punch into punch cups or rocks glasses. Carefully spoon ½ teaspoon of the grenadine over the back of a bar spoon and drip onto the top of each serving. Garnish with orange slices or a pineapple wedge and a pineapple leaf.

POMEGRANATE GRENADINE
MAKES ABOUT ¾ CUP

¾ cup demerara sugar

⅔ cup unsweetened pomegranate juice

1 orange twist

½ teaspoon pomegranate molasses (optional; see Note)

Place the sugar and pomegranate juice in a small saucepan over medium heat, and cook, stirring occasionally, until the sugar dissolves. Do not let boil. Add the orange twist and pomegranate molasses. Let cool completely, then strain through a fine-mesh sieve into a pint glass jar. Cover with a tight-fitting lid and refrigerate up to 1 month. Shake gently before using.

NOTE: Pomegranate molasses is available in Middle Eastern markets or online.

PEACH SANGRIA

Milton Williams, caterer to California stars, was a little bougie, and he knew it. In his 1981 cookbook, *The Party Book: Everything You Need to Know for Imaginative Never-Fail Entertaining at Home*, he complained that hosts living in Los Angeles didn't approve of fruit-alcohol concoctions served in a big bowl—unless the gathering was a party for young people or for the holidays. Sangria was approved for accompanying Mexican or Spanish meals, he said; otherwise, "punches look too chintzy, as though you're trying to save money."

Not so in the American South, where Peach Sangria made with fresh, juicy peaches and sweet wine was considered an expression of love and a way for a host to impress guests at a family gathering.

I'm from Los Angeles and I love Mexican food, so unlike Williams, I do indeed serve sangria, popular in Mexico as well as in Spain. I love red sangria during cooler months and this version of a sangria blanca on hot summer days. For my recipe, I tried a few tricks used in Italian Punch, a frozen peach-orange treat that appears in the rare and high-priced collection published in 1919, entitled *Pauline's Practical Book of the Culinary Art for Clubs, Home or Hotels.* (A first edition of this book was last listed at auction with an incredible starting bid of $13,500.) But to maintain its wine-punch pedigree, my summertime recipe bypasses canned and frozen fruit, and leans all the way into the sweet and juicy goodness of orchard-fresh white peaches, as recommended in the 2011 book *America I AM Pass It Down Cookbook: Over 130 Soul-Filled Recipes,* edited by Chef Jeff Henderson, with Ramin Ganeshram. Their Georgia White Peach Sangria is easy to personalize.

The mix begins with Pinot Grigio, but you can also stir in one-third off-dry or sweet Riesling to create an even sweeter base. Peach brandy is often called for, but there isn't a lot of it here, so good-quality brandy is just fine. Feel free to sweeten further with simple syrup or granulated sugar. I sometimes serve the drink with one of my Blackberry-Mint Ice Cubes (page 227) dropped into the glass along with regular ice cubes for a treat that tastes candy-coated. SERVES 6 OR 7

{recipe continues}

1 (750 ml) bottle Pinot Grigio

4 ounces (½ cup) peach schnapps

⅓ cup pineapple juice

1 ounce (2 tablespoons) brandy

1 ounce (2 tablespoons) triple sec or
homemade Tangerine Liqueur (page 37)

1 tablespoon lemon juice

1 cup lemon-lime soda, or to taste

Ice cubes

2 ripe white peaches, pitted and thinly sliced

18 to 21 seedless green grapes

2 tangerines, peeled and thinly sliced
crosswise

6 to 7 mint sprigs

In a large pitcher, combine the wine,
schnapps, pineapple juice, brandy, triple sec,
and lemon juice. Refrigerate until thoroughly
chilled, at least 4 hours.

Carefully stir in the soda, adding more
soda for a sweeter punch, if desired.

To serve, fill tall glasses halfway with
ice. Top each glass with 2 peach slices and
2 or 3 green grapes. Pour in the sangria and
garnish each drink with a tangerine slice and
mint sprig.

NOTE: As suggested above, for a sweeter
drink, add 1 or 2 Blackberry-Mint Ice Cubes
(page 227) to each cocktail glass along with
some regular ice.

ITALIAN PUNCH

*Put on stove in a saucepan 1 cup of water
and 2 cups sugar, stirring until sugar
is dissolved, cool, add ½ cup of lemon
juice, 1 cup orange juice and 1 quart of
peach pulp, prepared by rubbing canned
peaches through a fine sieve and adding
sufficient of syrup in can to thin, freeze,
serve in glasses.*

— Carrie Pauline Lynch, *Pauline's
Practical Book of the Culinary Art for
Clubs, Home or Hotels*, 1919

PEACH SANGRIA

STRAWBERRY WINE COOLER

Strawberry Wine Cooler, with its mild berry flavor, is my new favorite red drink for Juneteenth celebrations. I encountered the recipe in the Darden sisters' cookbook, *Spoonbread and Strawberry Wine: Recipes & Reminiscences of a Family*—part of a Fourth of July picnic menu that included roast suckling pig, fried chicken, barbecued spareribs, corn on the cob, greens, watermelon, ice cream, coconut cake, and a corn-beet-cucumber mix called Jubilee Salad. The recipe reminds me of old-school wine coolers, sipped on hot summer days by the pool.

There is no shortage of recipes in African American cookbooks for wine made from macerated cherries, blackberries, elderberries, muscadine grapes, and rose petals. (See Emily Meggett's Muscadine Wine on page 25.) The techniques described by some of the old-timey authors are especially enchanting, as you will hear in nineteenth-century baker and entrepreneur (and the first African American cookbook author) Malinda Russell's poetic instructions that follow in the sidebar.

If you don't have homemade Strawberry Wine (page 23) in your bar, you might substitute a mix of dry white wine (about 2 bottles, or 1.5 liters) and 1 cup homemade strawberry liqueur (page 44), but you really should try making your own; it's fun! SERVES 12 TO 14

---

1 large block of ice

1½ to 2 quarts homemade Strawberry Wine (page 23), chilled

¾ cup homemade Tangerine Liqueur (page 37), or 6 ounces (¾ cup) orange liqueur

1 (1-liter) bottle club soda or sparkling water

⅔ cup sliced fresh strawberries

Place the block of ice in a punch bowl and pour the wine and liqueur over it. Stir in the club soda until just mixed. Float the strawberries on top to garnish.

BLACKBERRY WINE

To one gallon berries pour over them one quart boiling water, crush the berries and strain through a hair sieve; add three pounds sugar to one gallon juice, turn into a stone pot and let it stand till through singing, skimming every morning; tie over the top a thin cloth, bottle and cork tight when through singing.

—Malinda Russell,
A Domestic Cook Book, 1866

BOWL OF EGGNOG

The secret to a great Tom and Jerry Cocktail is the batter; yes, it is a drink built on a thick base of creamed eggs and sugar. The paste is diluted with boiling water and a combination of spirits—rum, brandy, and whiskey. Traditionally, hosts serve it warm from a porcelain punch bowl in matching mugs that are inscribed "Tom and Jerry."

The traditional eggnog is a close cousin. Its beaten eggs and sugar foundation is also topped off with strong spirits, but here the liquid added is cold milk. In her 1939 recipe collection, *New Orleans Cookbook*, Creole chef Lena Richard provides recipes for both hot and cold eggnog on the same page.

Eggnog is a holiday tradition with myriad interpretations. In Baltimore Eggnog, the decadent Christmastime concoction is laced with madeira. Puerto Rican Coquito (page 80) gets tropical flavor from coconut and a jolt of sugar from sweetened condensed milk. Dark, molasses-based rum gives the creamy drink a sultry Jamaican vibe, while a splash of spiced rum laces the eggnog with hints of clove, ginger, and allspice.

Cato Alexander established a reputation as a gracious and welcoming host during the early nineteenth century. He was revered for the signature dishes on his menu at Cato's Tavern, in New York City. He also was a founding member of the New York African Society for Mutual Relief, which invested in real estate, as Juliet E. K. Walker explains in *The History of Black Business in America*. I salute him here for his expertise with Milk Punch and Virginia Eggnog—a drink so popular that he crafted it by the barrel.

Recipes for "a bowl eggnog" by Tom Bullock and Julian Anderson both also suggest the bartender habit of mixing eggnog in batches, by the gallon. To avoid food safety concerns, I have adapted their methods by lightly cooking the egg mixture and chilling the custard thoroughly. The chilling and storing for a day ahead before serving also allows the flavors to mellow. The billowy whipped cream is a luxurious alternative to the classic meringue crown.

And by all means, do as Edna Lewis and Scott Peacock suggest, in their 2003 book, *The Gift of Southern Cooking: Recipes and Revelations from Two Great American Cooks*: pack it into mason jars and deliver it to friends along with a tin of Christmas cookies. SERVES 8 TO 10

{recipe continues}

2 cups whole milk

2½ cups granulated sugar

10 large egg yolks, beaten

1 pint heavy whipping cream

16 ounces (2 cups) bourbon, or 8 ounces (1 cup) each bourbon and light rum

24 ounces (3 cups) brandy

Freshly grated nutmeg

In a medium saucepan, bring the milk to a simmer over medium-high heat, stirring occasionally to prevent scorching. Remove from the heat when bubbles begin to appear around the edges of the pan.

In a large bowl, using a whisk, beat the sugar and egg yolks until thickened, about 1 minute. Gradually stream about 1 cup of the hot milk into the egg mixture while whisking, then slowly whisk the tempered egg mixture into the remaining hot milk in the saucepan. (This will prevent the hot milk from curdling the eggs.)

Place the saucepan back on medium-low heat and cook, whisking constantly, 1 to 2 minutes, until the eggnog registers 160°F on an instant-read thermometer. Pour the custard into a clean bowl or pitcher, straining it through a fine-mesh sieve, if desired, to capture any cooked egg bits and to ensure a smooth texture. Stir in 1 cup of the cream, plus the bourbon and brandy. Let cool to room temperature, then cover and refrigerate at least 24 hours before serving to allow flavors to mellow.

In a large bowl, beat the remaining 1 cup cream with a wire whisk until soft peaks form. Gently spoon the whipped cream into the chilled eggnog. Serve in punch glasses or cups sprinkled with the nutmeg.

EGG NOG–COLD

1 pint milk

1 pint whipping cream

6 egg yolks

1 cup sugar

1 cup whiskey

2 teaspoons nutmeg

Beat egg yolks until light and lemon colored. Add sugar and continue to beat until thoroughly combined. Add the whiskey and one teaspoon nutmeg to the mixture. Add milk stirring well. Fold in stiffly beaten whipping cream. Sprinkle the top with the remaining nutmeg and serve.

EGG NOG–HOT

1 pint milk

1 pint whipping cream

6 egg yolks

4 egg whites

1 cup sugar

2 teaspoons nutmeg

Separate eggs, beat yolks until light. Add sugar and one teaspoon nutmeg, beat again. Heat milk and cream to boiling point. Add to sugar and egg mixture, cook 3 minutes. Whip egg whites until stiff, fold in while Egg Nog is still hot. Place a silver spoon in each glass and fill ¾ full of Egg Nog. Sprinkle a little of the remaining nutmeg in each glass. Flavor with whiskey to suit your taste.

—Lena Richard,
New Orleans Cook Book, 1939

COQUITO

In her 2022 breakout memoir and recipe collection, *Diasporican: A Puerto Rican Cookbook,* Illyanna Maisonet shares the origin story for Coquito, the luscious coconut eggnog that Puerto Rican families serve at Christmastime. The exact history was hard for the award-winning writer to track down, but she emerged with this: "The most common story goes that the first coquito was created with pitorro, a moonshine rum made from sugarcane and then buried underground to ferment. You would combine that with fresh coconut water and, later, grated coconut. You might also customize your pitorro with tropical fruits."

While this original drink sounds delicious and lean, contemporary recipes mostly feature sweetened, rich, full-fat coconut milk. I scoured other Puerto Rican cookbooks in my collection, including recipes by singer Kelis, by journalist Von Diaz, and by Yvonne Ortiz, who is author of one of the earliest celebrations of the island's cuisine, the 1997 book *A Taste of Puerto Rico: Traditional and New Dishes from the Puerto Rican Community.* I discovered Coquito formulas that blend several types of milk with white or gold Puerto Rican rum. Some whip in eggs or egg yolks to give the drink body. For others, warm spices are the key to luxurious richness.

As for the milks, coconut and sweetened condensed are constants, whereas using uber-sweet cream of coconut (Coco Lopez brand) and plain evaporated (dairy) milk are a matter of preference. I prefer the lighter taste of evaporated, but you can use what you like.

And, "if you want to go old-school with your coquito," Illyanna Maisonet says, "you might stick a piece of cheese, typically Edam, or what locals call *queso de bola,* in the finished bottle. The rum infuses the cheese, which you can then remove and serve with crackers when it's time to drink your coquito." SERVES 4 TO 6

---

1 (13½-ounce) can coconut milk

1 (14-ounce) can sweetened condensed milk

1 (12-ounce) can evaporated milk

Pinch of salt

6 ounces (¾ cup) light rum

6 ounces (¾ cup) dark rum

¼ teaspoon ground cinnamon, plus more for garnish

In a large pitcher, combine the coconut milk, condensed milk, evaporated milk, and salt. Stir well to thoroughly mix. Stir in the rums and cinnamon. Cover and refrigerate until cold, at least 8 hours. Serve sprinkled with additional cinnamon, if desired.

CHAPTER

BUILT

:::::

Taverns

TAVERNS

*I bought two glasses with one bit, and with the other three I bought
a jug of Geneva, nearly about three pints in measure. When we
came to Montserrat, I sold the gin for eight bits, and the tumblers for
two, so that my capital now amounted in all to a dollar. . . . I blessed
the Lord that I was so rich.*

—*Olaudah Equiano*, The Interesting Narrative of the Life of Olaudah
Equiano, or Gustavus Vassa, The African, *1789*

Enslaved African Olaudah Equiano's investments in the liquor business—
from the wine-making techniques he observed during palm wine production in Africa, to the business acumen he gained as a captive on an English
merchant's ship trading in Grenadian citrus fruits, sugar, and rum—eventually
enabled him to purchase his freedom, write an autobiography, and advocate for the
end of the British slave trade.

His enlightening first-person narrative of the Middle Passage exposed readers
to the horrors of captivity. But a closer look at his story also reveals the way that
African beverage makers preserved ancestral recipes—such as Guyanese "fly" made
from fermented potato or cassava, and "maubi," the Caribbean drink fermented
from tree bark—and monetized beverage businesses in the New World. Equiano is
an archetype of early American Black booze businesses.

While Equiano was trading in bootleg gin, free and enslaved Africans in colonial America were earning limited independence for themselves by operating
taverns, inns, and assembly halls where colonists, mostly men, learned news, discovered business opportunities, and refreshed themselves with food and drink.
Taverns and inns (as they were typically called in the Northeast) and ordinaries
(as they were generally called in the South) provided these services, with several
African American–owned establishments playing significant roles in the history of
hospitality—and more.

In the mid-eighteenth century, Philadelphia boasted approximately 120 licensed taverns, New York City about 220, and Boston around 115, Vaughn Scribner explains in *Inn Civility: Urban Taverns and Early American Civil Society.* The urban taverns validated masculine sensibilities and relegated women and "others" to the fringes of public society. Keepers of these critical communal spaces were usually well-off white men, even though the magistrates who approved their license applications knew that often the petitioner's wife or daughter would actually run the place.

In some towns and cities, prominent widows and white women of modest means, called middling women, openly operated taverns, but their licenses were still assigned to men. African and Native Americans were rarely granted tavern-keeping permits, but that didn't stop them from going into the business.

Unlicensed taverns were disparagingly called "disorderly houses." They catered to a less privileged clientele and often tolerated a mix of genders and races. They operated more humbly and in more remote locations than their high-class counterparts. And, Blacks, Native Americans, servants, and lower-class women, the supposed "societal inferiors," opened them. They were "the colonial version of a sketchy dive bar, places that didn't give a shit about fostering a proper tavern environment," Mallory O'Meara writes glibly in *Girly Drinks: A World History of Women and Alcohol.*

No doubt true in some or many instances, but this depiction still confused me when I considered portrayals of Cato Alexander's early 1800s tavern in several historical sources. According to cocktail historian Dave Wondrich, Cato, who was born enslaved, strategically opened his tavern in what is today midtown Manhattan, but was back then a ten-minute horse ride out of New York City, becoming a popular stop for the young men who liked to race their carriages. In doing so, Cato became "the first man to become famous" for making juleps and cocktails. Elise Lathrop's 1937 book, *Early American Inns and Taverns,* celebrates Cato's as "more fashionable" than similar resorts and roadhouses where New York socialites dined, drank tea, and enjoyed turtle feasts.

Another Black tavern keeper, Samuel "Black Sam" Fraunces, purchased a house in 1762 called Queen's Head in the southern tip of Manhattan—then the center of New York City. Its "Long Room" provided concerts and entertainment for "the best people of New York." Congressional delegations met at the tavern, and George Washington delivered his final speech to his troops there. When he advertised it for sale in 1775, Fraunces described the tavern this way: "The Queen's Head Tavern,

African and Native Americans were rarely granted tavernkeeping permits, but that didn't stop them from going into the business.

::::::

near the Exchange, is three stories high . . . with tile and lead roof, has 14 fireplaces, a most excellent large kitchen, fine dry cellars." It was an impressive place, not a smutty watering hole.

Leaders obviously desired the experience provided by Black tavernkeeps, but they simultaneously craved control over Black entrepreneurs too. After the Revolutionary War, Fraunces sold the tavern and became one of Washington's wage laborers, hired to act as steward and work in collaboration with the enslaved chef Hercules. As a condition of his employment, Fraunces was required to sign an agreement acknowledging that wine was forbidden at his table.

With these two figures in mind, I went searching for other self-sufficient Black booze businesses achieving success despite the limitations imposed on them. I discovered ambitious Black women who hid tavern activities in their boardinghouses, inns, hotels, coffeehouses, cookshops, confectionery stores, and eating places in response to enslavement, poverty, and disenfranchisement. They offered their own brand of hospitality in businesses, some operated legally, and others not.

In 1736, Mary Bernoon's clandestine whiskey distillery funded the oyster and ale house she operated in Providence, Rhode Island, with her husband, Emanuel. Nearly a century later, Black women were still trying to conduct business in the open. In 1819, five Black women paid $1,000 for permits to operate and sell liquor at taverns, cafés, and billiards halls, Juliet E. K. Walker notes in *The History of Black Business in America: Capitalism, Race, Entrepreneurship: Volume 1, To 1865.*

A Black woman entrepreneur finally claimed her flowers in 1890 when Mary Ellen "Mammy" Pleasant identified herself as "a capitalist" in the U.S. Census. A recipe collection published in 1970, *Mammy Pleasant's Cookbook,* is a flamboyant chronicle of her life told through dishes, stories, and American cities, from Nantucket, Boston, and Charleston to New Orleans and San Francisco. Pleasant was a cook, a laundress, a boardinghouse operator, and a conductor on the Underground Railroad. With the information she gleaned while doing this work, she acquired enormous wealth, which she used to fund abolitionist activities, support the Black press, and invest in real estate, but my favorite part of her story involves a saloon. In 1853, Pleasant joined the Athenaeum members of San Francisco's Black community, a group of leaders who convened to establish a social club and gathering place for African Americans. Guests would meet and socialize over drinks and games in the saloon, then retreat to a room upstairs for lectures, debates, and other intellectual activities, according to a 2012 City planning document referred to as the African American Citywide Historic Context Statement. They partied with purpose.

The drinks that follow in this chapter are built in a glass without shaking and with minimal stirring. To my mind, they seem befitting an older time of barkeeping. As the ice melts, your tastebuds are treated to different flavors. A mouthful of slightly diluted spirit will taste stronger than the next swallow, which might be more smooth as the mixer and melting ice gradually tame the alcohol's pungent essence.

I don't often make brand recommendations, but here it seems fitting. To turn these drinks from refreshment to homage, mix the rum-based recipes with Equiano Rum, the world's first African and Caribbean infusion to honor his spirit of freedom. When bourbon or whiskey is on the ingredients list, choose Uncle Nearest Premium Whiskey to salute the world's first-known African American master distiller, Nathan "Nearest" Green. He's the man believed to have invented the charcoal refining process that makes Tennessee whiskey unique, the hidden figure whose invention made his employer, Jack Daniels, a household name.

BLACKBERRY-GINGER BOURBON SMASH

The Smash cocktail is loosely defined as a mix of fruit, sweetener, strong spirit, and water served over ice. The fruit may be muddled as part of the spirit base or piled royally on top like a majestic crown. (To learn more about elaborate julep garnishes, turn to the history of the Hail-Storm on page 183.)

One intriguing confection was the Watermelon Smash I encountered in a 1994 book of recipes collected from Africa, the Caribbean, and the American South, entitled *A Traveler's Collection of Black Cooking*, by Yvonne M. Jenkins. But despite my excitement for an elaborate watermelon cocktail, I lost interest at the words "nonfat dry milk" in the ingredients.

The drink recipe I offer here harkens back to the ornately decorated Juleps and Smashes of old. I created it after encountering a delightful tale along with the recipe for a sweet, citrus-bourbon drink called "Lightning Calculator" in a 1942 collection, *Rebeccca's Cookbook*.

Rebecca West was a domestic worker who traveled the country and the world with her "lady," journalist and newspaper publisher Eleanor "Cissy" Patterson. West amassed and published a treasure trove of avant-garde recipes in a newspaper column—the first Black cooking column in a mainstream American newspaper.

West did not consume alcohol, so her cocktails chapter, which also includes compatible canapes, sources its drink recipes from two friends, "Old Alonzo" and George Young, the latter the chef at a prominent social club; she brags, "Not many, I do hear, can get ahead of him in cocktail receipts."

As the story goes, one of the ladies of the Club fell hard for an intoxicating lemon, orange juice, and powdered sugar mixture that Young muddled together, then shook with two jiggers of rye or bourbon, two egg whites, and ice for froth. Young topped off the mix with "some fizz from a siphon." The drink "looked about like pink lemonade. An didn taste any stronger," West reports. "But, you know, one of those ladies drank that lil drink and it put her out like that. . . . The ladies, was more interested in how they couldn't tell beforehand it was a strong cocktail. An Young, who sometime says quaint remarks, says, 'Well, I wraps my liquor round.'"

With West, George Young, the clubwomen, and seasonal fruit from the farmer's market as my muses, I endeavored to make a drink that "wraps the liquor round." I smashed sweet, ripe blackberries and a spicy homemade ginger syrup with lemon

{recipe continues}

juice and topped it off with bourbon and sparkling water, as you see here. If you prefer less kick and more floral aroma, swap St-Germain elderflower liqueur for the ginger syrup and exchange the sparkling water with ginger beer. Float a half teaspoon of beautifully purple Empress gin over the top to make this drink a bright beauty. SERVES 1

5 large fresh blackberries

1 tablespoon Ginger Syrup (recipe follows), or ½ ounce (1 tablespoon) St-Germain elderflower liqueur

1 tablespoon fresh lemon juice

2 ounces (¼ cup) bourbon

Crushed ice (see page 184)

¼ cup sparkling water (or ginger beer, if using St-Germain)

½ teaspoon Empress Indigo gin (optional)

1 mint sprig

Place 3 berries, the ginger syrup or liqueur, and the lemon juice in a rocks glass. Use a muddler to gently mash and mix until the berries release their juice, about 10 seconds. Add the bourbon and fill the glass with crushed ice. Pour in the sparkling water or ginger beer. Float the gin on top, if you'd like, and garnish with the mint and remaining berries.

VARIATION: For a clean drink, place the berries and ginger syrup in a cocktail shaker. Use a muddler or a wooden spoon to gently mix until the berries release their juice, about 10 seconds. Add the lemon juice and bourbon, and fill with crushed ice. Shake until cold, about 10 seconds. Use a cocktail strainer to strain the drink into a rocks cocktail glass filled with crushed ice. Top with the ginger beer and garnish with the remaining berries or the mint sprig.

GINGER SYRUP
MAKES 1½ CUPS

1 cup granulated sugar

1 cup water

½ cup (2 ounces) thinly sliced fresh ginger (not necessary to peel)

1 tablespoon minced jalapeño chile, optional

In a small saucepan over high heat, bring the sugar, water, and ginger to a boil. Boil for 1 minute. Remove from the heat. Stir in the chile pepper if using, then let cool. Strain the syrup through cheesecloth, transfer to a pint glass jar, cover, and refrigerate for up to 1 month.

FANCY WHISKEY SMASH

Fill large Bar glass ½ full Shaved Ice.

2 teaspoonfuls Bar Sugar

3 sprigs Mint pressed with muddler in 1 Jigger aerated Water

1 Jigger whiskey

Stir well; strain into Sour glass; dress with Fruit and serve.

—Tom Bullock, *The Ideal Bartender*, 1917

PINEAPPLE-LEMON HIGHBALL

It is virtually impossible today to order a highball without getting the side eye from your bartender. That's because the word is an old-fashioned way of asking for a drink made with whiskey, scotch, or bourbon, poured over ice and crowned with a mixer like soda or ginger ale. The more popular way to order it is to say, "scotch and . . ." or "bourbon and . . ."

Barmasters have embraced the familiar combination in many ways since the pre-Prohibition days. When I'm in the bar, I often order a Ranch Water (tequila and Topo Chico sparkling mineral water with squeeze of lime) or I gravitate toward whatever grapefruit concoction they have with a fancy name that is essentially alcohol and ruby red grapefruit juice; you get the picture.

This version breaks a few rules, comingling ingredients and techniques from two classics: Tom Bullock's High Ball and the playful Horse's Neck. Before the Y peeler was invented, the Horse's Neck demonstrated a bartender's skill with a small knife. The drink is made with whiskey, ginger ale, and ice, and is garnished with a long spiral or ribbon of lemon peel that snakes around the inside of and over the rim of the glass.

I started my recipe development by tinkering with two versions of the Horse's Neck, one crafted by early mixologist Julian Anderson, the other a simple mixture from midcentury cook and author Rebecca West. Both drinks turned out sweet and fizzy, with a faint bite from ginger ale. Next, I fiddled with Bullock's version of the Admiral Schley High Ball. His choice of Angelica liqueur, Sweet Catawba wine, or Tokay dessert wine in combination with soda and pineapple syrup brought out the fruit-forward sweetness of the wine. As an alternative, I like Lillet Blanc aperitif for its floral notes, and I make my own pineapple syrup to amplify the cocktail's bright, clean, fruity freshness. (You can also make this syrup with berries, peaches, or apricots, all of which would be delicious.) To garnish the drink, squeeze the oils from the lemon peel onto the rim of the glass before dropping the twist into the drink. SERVES 1

{recipe continues}

Ice cubes

1¾ to 2 ounces (3½ to 4 tablespoons) Irish whiskey

1¾ ounces (3½ tablespoons) sweet white dessert wine

½ tablespoon fresh lemon juice

½ tablespoon Pineapple Syrup (recipe follows)

½ cup seltzer or sparkling water

Lemon twist or strip of lemon peel

Fill a highball glass halfway with ice. Pour in the whiskey, wine, lemon juice, and pineapple syrup. Fill the glass with the seltzer. Squeeze the lemon twist over the drink, then drop it into the glass to serve.

PINEAPPLE SYRUP

MAKES ABOUT I CUP

1½ cups chopped fresh pineapple, in ½-inch pieces

⅔ cup granulated sugar

⅔ cup water

Pinch of salt

In a medium saucepan, combine the pineapple and sugar. Stir to thoroughly coat the fruit with the sugar, then let stand 3 hours or overnight, until the sugar is dissolved and the fruit is syrupy. Stir in the water and salt, and simmer over medium heat for 2 minutes, just to completely dissolve the sugar. Strain the syrup through cheesecloth, then transfer to a half-pint glass jar, cover tightly, and refrigerate for up to 1 month. (If desired, serve the remaining pineapple pulp over ice cream or stir it into plain yogurt for a treat.)

HORSE'S NECK

Use a large glass. Cut rind of whole lemon in one long string. Place in glass with one end hanging over the rim, three lumps of ice, one drink of rye whiskey. Fill glass with ginger ale and serve.

—Rebecca West, *Rebecca's Cookbook*, 1942

PINEAPPLE-LEMON HIGHBALL

CIDER CUP

This is an excellent and refreshing summer drink, made extra special by the aromatic and vegetal notes of mint and cucumber. It is a less-sweet, fizzier take on mixologist Julian Anderson's version of the classic Cider Cup, a delightful cocktail made by mixing brandy and white Curaçao with hard cider. Hard cider virtually disappeared from the bar following Prohibition, but it has come back strong thanks to today's interest in craft brewing. You may also see the vintage drink reworked with wine or Champagne.

Choose your cider according to personal taste; ciders range from sweet to dry, and depending on the style, can be very apple-forward or taste more like yeasty funk. The brandy is subtle here, masked by the brightness of the generous fruit garnish. Club soda aerates the drink and gives it a bit of a head.

This Cider Cup is not just a scrumptious libation; it is also a way to honor women and the enslaved Africans who were cider-making experts. In Chesapeake households from the late seventeenth to the late eighteenth century, beverage making was part of a woman's household cooking chores. She produced fermented ciders from apples, peaches, and persimmons; made molasses "beer" concoctions with molasses, water, and yeast; brewed a little unhopped ale from corn and molasses; and distilled some apple brandy from cider in primitive stills, as Sarah Hand Meacham explains in her 2009 book, *Every Home a Distillery: Alcohol, Gender, and Technology in the Colonial Chesapeake.*

Raise a glass to these unsung masters when you enjoy this drink. SERVES 2 TO 4

---

1 medium cucumber

Juice of 1 lemon

1 ounce (2 tablespoons) white Curaçao, or 2 tablespoons homemade Tangerine Liqueur (page 37)

1 ounce (2 tablespoons) brandy

16 ounces (2 cups) hard apple cider

2 orange slices

2 lemon slices

1 cup club soda

2 to 4 small fresh mint sprigs

With a vegetable peeler, cut two 1-inch-wide strips of peel from the cucumber. Place the peels in a pitcher, and reserve the cucumber for another use. Add the lemon juice, Curaçao, brandy, cider, and orange and lemon slices. Refrigerate, covered, for 3 hours, or until thoroughly chilled.

Stir in the club soda, then pour into tall glasses and garnish with the mint.

CIDER CUP

(Use a Pitcher)

2 Tablespoonsful fine sugar;

dissolve in a little water;

add the juice of one lemon;

1 Pony White Curacao;

½ Pony brandy;

1 Pint of cider;

1 Bottle of plain soda;

2 slices of orange;

2 slices of lemon;

1 Cucumber rind;

a few lumps of clear ice;

stir until cold; top off with a few sprigs of fresh mint with the stems down.

Serve.

—Julian Anderson,
Julian's Recipes, 1919

CUBA LIBRE

If you have sipped Rum and Coke, you have enjoyed a Cuba Libre, a highball that takes its name from a mid-nineteenth-century expression adopted by Cubans fighting for their independence from Spain. Soldiers sipped a mix of honey or molasses, water, and rum. The story goes that, sometime after the Spanish-American war in 1898, an American soldier was in a Havana bar, mixed his rum with a Coca-Cola and lime, and shouted, *"¡Por Cuba libre!"* Whether it was the combination or the slogan that caught on, this drink has been a staple ever since.

There's a racist side to the history of this drink, too. But—whether we're talking about the marketing tactics that cola manufacturers employed to segregate their products during the mid-twentieth century, or the history of enslavement, Caribbean colonization, and the excesses of plantation hospitality associated with rum, none of these events have changed this drink's appeal in African American bar culture. Perhaps that's because "Rum is the sacramental wine of the New World. African-Inspired religions of the hemisphere use the sugarcane spirit to lubricate ceremonies and celebrate life," as Jessica B. Harris reminds us in her 2010 book, *Rum Drinks: 50 Caribbean Cocktails, from Cuba Libre to Rum Daisy*.

But let's get back to making the beverage.

Dark or spiced rums may be substituted for light rum, and sugar-free soda for the classic cola, to suit your preference. And if you're in the mood for a drink that screams revolution, try T-Pain's revision; his Fly Away adds a splash of butterscotch schnapps and a few drops of orange-flower water, and tops everything off with cherry cola. Yes, the superstar rapper is an avid cocktailian, as evidenced by his 2021 book, *Can I Mix You a Drink?*

A Hurricane or cola glass, either of which has a bell-like curve, allows the carbonation to move throughout the glass, making the cocktail balanced without the need to stir or shake. The lime squeeze is a must. SERVES 1

Crushed ice (see page 184)

Juice of 1 lime, about 2 tablespoons

1½ to 2 ounces (3 to 4 tablespoons) white rum

4 ounces (½ cup) cola

Fill a tall Hurricane or cola glass two-thirds full with the crushed ice. Use back of a bar spoon to pour the lime juice over the ice, flavoring the ice. Add the rum and top with the cola.

HIBISCUS GIN RICKEY

The Rickey is a highball made with rum, gin, or bourbon, plus lime juice and carbonated water. It provides fizzy refreshment without a sweetener or mixer.

Tom Bullock offered two Rickeys in his 1917 recipe collection. The Carleton Rickey–St. Louis Style is a mix of lime juice, whiskey, and sweet soda; to make the Rickey "Royal," Bullock stirred together gin, raspberry syrup, vermouth, and ginger ale, then dressed the whole thing with fruit. Julian Anderson's approach, in print two years later, was the standard one and had this tip: "Serve with a spoon in the glass." Other Rickeys followed, including a very modest recipe by Sarah Helen Mahammitt. In 1939, after thirty years of catering and teaching cooking, she published a spiral-bound manual of tested recipes, which she divided into different sections for novice and advanced cooks, for rules and guidelines for domestics, and for instructions for general catering, "in hope that it will prove beneficial to all whom it may reach." Her Rickey, perhaps geared toward sharing knowledge of fundamental recipes, is as simple as they come: gin, lime, soda.

Fast-forward to a modern adaptation of that approach, which comes by way of Matthew Raiford's 2021 book, *Bress 'n' Nyam: Gullah Geechee Recipes from a Sixth-Generation Farmer.* He and Jovan Sage partnered with Simple Man Distillery to create a hibiscus-flavored gin with enhanced botanical notes and "a whisper of pink and bold, clean flavors." You can make this drink special, even without Gullah Geechee gin; just add a splash of bright and sweetly spiced tart Sorrel (page 34). SERVES 1

Ice cubes

3½ tablespoons lime juice

1½ ounces (3 tablespoons) light rum, bourbon, or gin

¼ cup club soda or sparkling water

Sorrel (page 34), to taste

1 lime wheel

Fill a highball glass halfway with ice cubes. Add the lime juice and spirit of choice. Top off with the club soda and the Sorrel. Garnish with the lime wheel.

GIN RICKEY

Serve in water glass.

1 glass of gin

½ lime

Fill with sparkling water and cubed ice. Stir and stir well.

—Sarah Helen Mahammitt,
*Recipes and Domestic Service:
The Mahammitt School of Cookery,* 1939

OLD FASHIONED

The Old Fashioned is a standard cocktail that is built in the glass by pouring in whiskey, bitters, water, and sugar, then garnishing with citrus and a cherry. The recipe is commonplace throughout African American cookbook history.

Cleora Butler's 1985 book, *Cleora's Kitchens: The Memoir of a Cook & Eight Decades of Great American Food*, one of my favorite books for storytelling and recipes, remembers the drink classically in the chapter celebrating "The Twenties."

I took inspiration for the following recipe from a 2000 book, *The New Low-Country Cooking: 125 Recipes for Coastal Southern Cooking with Innovative Style*. There, chef Marvin Woods muddles the orange slice, cherry, bitters, and sparkling water with simple syrup until blended, then tops the drink with a generous amount of ice and finishes it off with bourbon.

Muddling the fruit with sugar and filling the glass with crushed ice makes a great Old Fashioned. But if you splurge on Luxardo's maraschino cherries, don't muddle them. These pricey dark globes taste deep and complex, and are worth enjoying whole—nothing like the fire-engine-red candy-like garnish we grew up fishing up from the bottom of a Shirley Temple. Whiskey connoisseurs may prefer to build this drink in a glass over an ice ball or large ice cubes, which melt more slowly than crushed ice. SERVES 1

---

1 sugar cube or 2 teaspoons demerara sugar

2 dashes Angostura bitters (about 5 drops)

1 lemon, lime, or orange twist

1 tablespoon water

2½ ounces (5 tablespoons) bourbon

Crushed ice (see page 184) or ice cubes

1 Luxardo maraschino cherry

Place the sugar, bitters, lemon twist, and water in a rocks glass. Muddle to crush lightly. Add the bourbon. Fill the glass to the top with the ice. Garnish with a skewered cherry.

BELLINI

Nashville poet Caroline Randall Williams and her mother, author and hit country songwriter Alice Randall, tell us in their 2015 cookbook, *Soul Food Love*, that drinking this peach and sparkling wine combo—a favorite of Ernest Hemingway's—wasn't just for iconic writers.

Starting in the late nineteenth century, African American women established service organizations that worked to uplift their communities. They held their own conventions, published cookbooks as fundraising projects, and gathered in private homes to set economic, social, and political priorities. This work continues to this day.

At clubwomen's brunches, the Randalls (iconic writers and activists in their own right) encountered the Bellini made with peaches canned in heavy syrup; some that included an additional alcohol to the prosecco, usually peach schnapps or Grand Marnier (or brandy); others that muddled a single peach with ½ cup of sugar; still others that were refreshed with orange juice; and many that were laced with simple syrup.

This is the mother-daughter duo's recipe: simple, classic, and best made in the peak of the summer peach season, when the fruit gives way with just the slightest bit of crushing. SERVES I

¼ **ripe peach, peeled and chopped, plus 1 thin slice reserved for garnish**

½ **teaspoon honey**

¾ **cup prosecco or other dry sparkling wine, cold**

With a muddler or a spoon, muddle the peach with the honey in a cocktail glass until pureed. Pour the peach puree into a Champagne flute. Top with the prosecco, and garnish with the peach slice.

GINGER SUNRISE

I knew I had to try the simple syrup spiked with hot chile and ginger the moment I saw it in the 2018 cookbook *Carla Hall's Soul Food: Everyday and Celebration*. With the chef and food television icon's recipe as my jumping-off point, I started searching other Black cookbooks for drink inspirations to use it in. This drink, which leans into a spicy syrup's interplay with rum, is the result. For that tingle of heat, adding the optional chile pepper to my Ginger Syrup (page 90) is a must here.

SERVES I

Ice cubes

1 ounce (2 tablespoons) fresh orange juice

½ ounce (1 tablespoon) fresh lime juice

2 ounces (4 tablespoons) light or dark rum

2 ounces (¼ cup) Ginger Syrup (page 90)

1 teaspoon maraschino cherry juice

Sparkling water, as needed

1 orange wheel

1 maraschino cherry

Fill a tall Collins glass halfway with ice. Add the orange and lime juices, then pour in the rum. Stir in the syrup, then add the cherry juice. Stir once with a bar spoon or swizzle stick. Top the drink with sparkling water, and garnish with the orange wheel and cherry.

LAYERED

Mixologists

MIXOLOGISTS

*The art of mixing liquors has come to be a highly respectable and
profitable calling and men of excellent repute are found in its ranks.
To protect the better grade of workmen from the shiftless and
unreliable, and to stimulate a broader spirit of fraternity, an
organization was found necessary.*

—The Colored American, *1900*

One of my first questions about the art of cocktail mixing involved the layering technique. What is it, and can it be achieved at home without a fully stocked bar? The answer put the skills of the Colored Mixologists Club on full display. And the above quote about the Club, published in Washington, DC's weekly African American newspaper, *The Colored American,* added another piece to the puzzling mixed messages surrounding Black people and booze.

The paper, which published from 1893 to 1904, distinguished itself as a national publication highlighting the achievements of African Americans across the country. Its original articles were contributed by prominent Black journalists, and its themes routinely focused on religion, politics, education, military affairs, and Black fraternal organizations "rather than relying on boiler-plate, filler material taken from other publications," according to the overview of the newspaper's archive at the Library of Congress, where I viewed its pages.

On November 10, 1900, *The Colored American* published a profile of the Mixologists Club, an organization formed in 1898 in Washington, DC, by R. R. Bowie, J. Burke Edelin, and others. Illustrations accompanied member biographies, as did details about their second annual ball. The story opened poetically with a pseudo headline and a long summary of what was to come: "An Aggregation of Energetic Young Bonifaces who Find Time Between Smiles to Woo the Goddess of Mirth— Their Annual Ball to be a Brilliant Function—Notes of the Organization and Facts About its Officers and Members—'What's Yours, Gentlemen?'"

This elaborate intro was followed by information about the organization, its officers, and details on the upcoming event, which was expected to be a momentous occasion. "Everybody and his fair partner is expected to be present," the story declared.

The article drew a clear distinction between bartenders and mixologists, elevating the skill and knowledge of the latter beyond simply mixing drinks as ordered. Understanding the elements of good customer service was also essential to business success. In other words, mixologists were thinking men.

> *As its name indicates [the Mixologists Club] is made up principally*
> *of the very useful gentlemen who tickle the popular palate with*
> *artistic combinations of the "fluid that cheers" who are wont to talk*
> *entertainingly of the weather, the drama, the ring, the track, or politics*
> *while shoveling in the cracked ice or putting the finishing touches upon*
> *a "Mamie Taylor," a "Manhattan" or a "Rickey."*
>
> *The antiquated bartender, with his unkept hair and dingy linen, is*
> *no longer seen in first class resorts. In his stead has come the up to date*
> *business man, spick span in cleanly attire, polite and affable, alert and*
> *progressive, with a marvelous insight into that mysterious realm we*
> *call human nature. He knows how to "make good" for the "house" and*
> *builds around his engaging personality a "trade" that is all his own. . . .*
> *In response to this plain necessity there sprung up the Mixologist Club,*
> *and at once its roll began to scintillate the stars of the restaurant world*
> *all of the solid young men of the craft rallied under its banner.*

Thus, the Mixologists Club's presence declared Black agency, promoting solidarity and industry excellence while supporting the community through activism and property ownership. In so doing, the fraternity also provided a form of grass-roots protection from D.C.'s segregationist policies for the surprising number of Black professionals perfecting their skills behind the bar. These specialists left their own unique marks on the private club and bar industry, between 1820 and Prohibition, an era when Black people's "proximity to liquor was frequently—and unjustly—associated with lawlessness and vice," as Dave Wondrich has noted in articles written and speeches given about the Club.

Less than twenty years later, two professionals claimed their expertise by publishing books that preserved their knowledge for generations to come.

Julian Anderson's 1919 collection, *Julian's Recipes: In Remembrance of Olden Times,* is the second work to limit its recipes exclusively to mixed drinks, following Tom Bullock's *The Ideal Bartender,* published in 1917. Anderson crafted classic cocktails at The Montana Club, an exclusive men's social club in Helena, Montana, and grew the mint for his mint juleps in his own backyard.

In addition to classic mixed drink formulas that paint a fuller portrait of African American bar mastery, Bullock and Anderson specialized in craft cocktails, and importantly, the layered ones that I went searching for.

A layered cocktail, sometimes known as a "stacked" drink or a "pousse café," relies on the slightly different densities of various liquors to create colored layers in the glass—anywhere from two to seven—often enjoyed through a straw, one liqueur at a time. The name *pousse café* means "to push down the coffee," a reference to drinks served after dinner and the coffee course.

The Mixologists Club's presence declared Black agency, promoting solidarity and industry excellence while supporting the community through activism and property ownership.

Making a successful layered cocktail requires more than a steady hand to float the liqueurs on top of one another. You also have to know the specific densities of the various ingredients and then put them in the glass in the right order. The technique is similar to the bartender trick of floating the final ingredient—usually a high-proof spirit or a particularly colorful liqueur—which Tiffanie Barriere and Brandon Tipton, the bartenders who taught me so much about cocktail making for this book, say is primarily for looks, although it also enhances the aroma and first sip by leaving the floated ingredient near the surface.

The effect of the layers, though, is meant to be colorful, delicious, and dramatic. See for yourself.

BLACK VELVET, PAGE 119

POUSSE CAFÉ

The Pousse Café is a show-stopping drink that is pure dessert in a glass, an iconic after-dinner drink. To make it, you carefully pour an assortment of liqueurs over an upside-down bar spoon placed over the glass to create a stunning rainbow. You begin the process with room-temperature ingredients; this helps them layer better and accentuates each's unique character. I stay close to recipes published by mixologists Tom Bullock and Julian Anderson to ensure that the layers have a proper difference in viscosity. If the ingredients do mix a little, give the drink a gentle stir and be proud of your efforts. And don't be afraid to try again.

To my surprise, the 50th Anniversary edition of *Mr. Boston: Official Bartender's Guide* calls its Pousse-Café the "Aunt Jemima," named after the pancake mix that until recently bore the image of a Black female cook. Why one would title a drink that layers "five-star" brandy with white crème de cacao and Benedictine this way is anyone's guess. If I were going to make the Mr. Boston version to honor the women whose images are memorialized by the Aunt Jemima name, I would reclaim the drink by using brown crème de cacao. But that is another story. SERVES 1

½ tablespoon raspberry syrup

½ tablespoon maraschino syrup

½ tablespoon vanilla syrup

¼ ounce (½ tablespoon) Curaçao

¼ ounce (½ tablespoon) Green Chartreuse

¼ ounce (½ tablespoon) brandy

Use a bar spoon to place the raspberry syrup in a small sherry glass. Add the maraschino syrup by slowly pouring it over the back side of the bar spoon set close to the raspberry syrup. Repeat with the remaining liquids, starting with the vanilla syrup, then the Curaçao, then the Chartreuse, and finally the brandy. Serve with a straw.

SANTINAS POUSSE CAFE

Use a Small Straight Brandy Glass

1/3 Maraschino;

1/3 Curacao (Red);

1/3 Brandy; and serve.

This drink is generally served after a cup of black coffee.

—Julian Anderson,
Julian's Recipes, 1919

ANGEL'S TIP

In Julian Anderson's *Julian's Recipes*—the second cocktail recipe collection to be published by a Black man—a sweet layering of anisette liqueur, the violet-infused Crème de Yvette, and citrusy Curaçao goes by the provocative name "Angel's Tit." The drink—and the name—has evolved a lot since then. Order an Angel's Tip today, and you will probably be served a chocolate-cherry concoction, possibly shaken with cream instead of being layered.

The following recipe brings us back to Julian's original, layering in the ingredients for a beautiful presentation. You can substitute crème de violette for the Yvette; both are made with violet petals, but berries, honey, and orange peel are part of what makes the Yvette unique (and more expensive). Please resist the temptation to swap the drier triple sec for the sweet and fruity Curaçao. My homemade Tangerine Liqueur (page 37) will add a nice, nuanced citrus flavor, though. During the summer, I like to trade gin for the anisette, and add the juice of half a lemon for a delicate poolside refresher. SERVES 1

1 maraschino cherry

1 ounce (2 tablespoons) anisette liqueur

1 ounce (2 tablespoons) Crème de Yvette or crème de violette

1 ounce (2 tablespoons) Curaçao, or 2 tablespoons homemade Tangerine Liqueur (page 37)

1½ teaspoons (1 bar spoon) heavy whipping cream

Place the maraschino cherry in a sherry glass. With a bar spoon, slowly add the anisette to the glass. Use the bar spoon to carefully layer the Crème de Yvette on top of the anisette, pouring it in slowly. Carefully and slowly, use the bar spoon also to add the Curaçao to the glass. Finally, use the bar spoon to top the drink with the cream. Serve with a straw.

ARF AND ARF

This simple layered drink is made with just two ingredients: ale and porter. It is generally served chilled from the tap in America, and may be served at room temperature in Europe. It is sometimes known as the Black and Tan or the Half and Half in today's bar speak. And it is delicious layered with Guinness Stout (Irish, thick, coffee-like, malted sweet) and Bass Pale Ale (English, tan in color, light).

Pour this drink and raise a toast to Peter Hemings, thought to be America's first craft brewer, according to researchers at the historic site of Monticello, Thomas Jefferson's home. Peter, whose brother James was Jefferson's respected, French-trained chef, was also known to be proficient in French cookery. The Monticello website explains Peter's brewing skills this way:

> In 1813, Captain Joseph Miller, a British brewmaster, successfully taught Hemings how to malt and brew beer; Jefferson wrote that, "Peter's brewing of the last season I am in hopes will prove excellent . . . the only cask of it we have tried proves so."

If you want to take the Hemings homage a step further, mix this drink with Monticello, a barrel-fermented beer that has persimmon puree added. The latter was created by Avery Brewing, in Boulder, Colorado, following an 1822 recipe from Monticello; it was produced as part of its Ales of Antiquity series. The company hopes that sharing Hemings's story will give him the "credit and recognition he deserves."

Set the mood and sip the drink to the up-tempo classic, Duke Ellington's "Black and Tan Fantasy." SERVES 1

---

1 cup (8 ounces) ale

1 cup (8 ounces) porter

Tilt a tall glass 45 degrees and gradually pour the ale into the glass to avoid a head or foam. To layer the porter, hold a bar spoon upside down over the glass. Slowly and carefully pour the porter over the back of the spoon so that it drops lightly into the glass. This step reduces the mixing and encourages the porter to float on top.

GRAPEFRUIT WHISKEY COCKTAIL

For collectors, the price of a 1934 pocket-sized cocktail recipe booklet titled *How to Make Old Kentucky Famed Drinks* soared after cocktail authority Dave Wondrich wrote that it contained a heretofore forgotten Black bartender's photo and recipes. Wondrich paid a few bucks for his copy; mine cost as much as a fancy dinner.

"There's a photo of a man—a Black man—wielding a silver three-piece cocktail shaker," Wondrich observes in his article for the Daily Beast. 'Prince—Head Bartender, Wynn-Stay Club, Louisville,' the caption reads. On the facing page is 'Prince's own recipe' for the Wynn-Stay Club Whisky Sour, and the following page has the Wynn-Stay Club Whisky Cocktail. And that's all the information we get, not even the man's last name."

Wondrich learned that Prince Herbert Martin was born in Franklin, Kentucky, on Valentine's Day, 1895. He held bellman and waiter jobs before joining the staff at the Wynn-Stay Club, performing the duties of bartender, caterer, and steward. And he is one of just two barmen identified in the booklet, which was published by the Brown, Forman Distillery Company in Louisville, Kentucky.

A blend of grapefruit juice, honey, and whiskey—the De Rigueur—followed Martin's recipes in a section named "Cocktails for the Ladies." I was eager to re-imagine the B-F recipe for modern tastes, so it was time to tinker. For reference, I considered the grapefruit-whiskey combination mixed in Tamika Hall and Colin Asare-Appiah's *Black Mixcellence: A Comprehensive Guide to Black Mixology*.

The drink I suggest here is made with Ruby Red grapefruit, my favorite. You can juice pink grapefruit too, but you will want to lace the drink with a drizzle of honey for earthy sweetness. For bright color, choose ½ teaspoon of my homemade grenadine (page 73) or maraschino cherry juice. You can even dissolve granulated sugar in water and dash in some orange bitters for a cocktail that is smooth and fragrant, an homage to Black mixologists like Prince Martin. SERVES 1

---

2 ounces (4 tablespoons) whiskey

1 ounce (2 tablespoons) Ruby Red grapefruit juice

Juice of ½ lime

½ teaspoon honey, optional

1 dried grapefruit wheel

Fill a rocks glass half full with ice cubes. Add the whiskey and juices. Using the back of a bar spoon, drizzle the honey over the drink, if desired. Do not stir. Garnish with the dried grapefruit wheel and serve.

BLACK VELVET

Here is another striped drink from yesteryear that is experiencing a renaissance. Known as the Black Velvet, it combines the smooth texture of a dark beer with the effervescent viscosity of Champagne. If you're worried this drink will seem too old-fashioned for your guests, don't be. Rapper T-Pain, who published a 2021 drinks book based on his songs, entitled *Can I Mix You a Drink? 50 Cocktails from My Life & Career*, offers a modern rendition he calls "I'm So Hood." The cocktail is made with cognac, lemon juice, Moët & Chandon Champagne, and a twist on the beer in the form of an "Old English reduction"—Olde English Malt Liquor that has been simmered with sugar and spices until syrupy.

My simple version (see photograph on page 111), adapted from Tom Bullock's Black and Tan Punch, will get you started. A goblet is not essential, but it does help give the drink balance by providing plenty of room for both liquids. Using a bar spoon to add the porter to the Champagne already in the glass will create beautiful layers. Also, try making this drink with a Guinness Stout in place of the porter for more contrast and a flavorful punch. SERVES 1

4 ounces (½ cup) chilled Champagne

4 ounces (½ cup) cold porter

Tilt a goblet 45 degrees and gradually pour the chilled Champagne into the glass to avoid a head or foam. To layer on the porter, hold a bar spoon upside down over the glass. Slowly and carefully pour the porter over the back of the spoon so that it drops lightly into the glass. This step reduces mixing and encourages the liquids to separate. Serve immediately.

BLACK AND TAN PUNCH

For party of 10

1 lb white Sugar.

Juice of 6 Lemons

1 quart Guinness Stout.

1 quart Champagne.

Pour mixture of Lemon Juice and Sugar in the Champagne and Stout, ice cold. Serve in Punch glasses dressed with Fruit.

—Tom Bullock, *The Ideal Bartender*, 1917

COGNAC, COFFEE, AND CREAM

Long before rap star Busta Rhymes chanted "Pass the Courvoisier" and 2Pac dropped an entire rhyme about the glory of Hennessy, African Americans were sipping barrel-aged brandy neat, on the rocks, and mixed into cocktails. Several drinks we now think of as classic combos emerged during the 1980s, when spirits companies competed for the attention of African American imbibers by placing seductive ads in magazines like *Ebony* and *Jet*.

Two alluring images of Black couples living the good life come to mind: one, a Canadian Club promo featuring a stunningly beautiful schoolmate of mine; the other, a persuasive campaign for Kahlúa that whipped the Mexican coffee liqueur, cognac, and cream into an enticing mocha cocktail. The caption, "Do something delicious tonight," summarized the invitation.

Rapper and author T-Pain revives this sexy spirit with a modernized coffee cocktail called the "Up Down." Featuring coffee liqueur, cognac, coconut milk, and cardamom bitters, the dessert drink is prepared shaken in his 2021 recipe book, *Can I Mix You a Drink? 50 Cocktails from My Life & Career*.

For my version, I took a cue from another classic, the White Russian, and I layered something like the creamy, coffee mocha cocktail Kahlúa advertised, using my homemade coffee liqueur. SERVES 1

Ice cubes

2 tablespoons homemade Coffee Liqueur (page 28)

2 ounces (¼ cup) cognac

2 tablespoons heavy cream, milk, or non-dairy milk

Fill a cocktail glass two-thirds full with ice. Using the back of a bar spoon, carefully and slowly pour in the liqueur. Repeat with the cognac and then with the cream to create a layered look. Do not stir before serving.

RUM AND GINGER BEER

The "Dark 'n' Stormy" is a beautiful drink from Bermuda that features a deep, dark rum base topped with an amber layer of ginger beer and a squeeze of lime juice. Legends regarding its origins abound, but one fact is known: the name of the drink itself is a registered trademark, and the official recipe calls for Gosling's Black Seal Bermuda Black Rum and their brand of ginger beer as well.

For my version, I was inspired by two recipes for this drink—one from Tanya Holland's 2014 cookbook, *Brown Sugar Kitchen*, and the other from Marcus Samuelsson's 2016 book, *The Red Rooster Cookbook*. Both layer the dark rum with homemade ginger beer and lime juice, but Marcus's Dark and Stormier mellows the ginger bite with a little simple syrup. Rather than a little lime wedge, this recipe includes a significant amount of lime juice, for extra zing. And while my homemade ginger beer (page 41) isn't effervescent, feel free to add a splash of soda water for bubbles. Either way, the drink is pure perfection, served alongside a bowl of fish chowder. SERVES 1

Ice cubes

2 ounces (¼ cup) dark rum

2 tablespoons fresh lime juice

1 teaspoon Simple Syrup (page 31)

¼ cup homemade Ginger Beer (page 41)

1 lime wedge

Fill a Collins glass two-thirds full with ice. Add the rum, followed by the lime juice and syrup. Stir once or twice with a swizzle stick, then carefully pour the ginger beer into the glass. Garnish with the lime wedge and serve immediately.

CHARDONNAY AND CHAMBORD

Kir Royale is an elegant cocktail built in a fluted Champagne glass. It is made by pouring black currant liqueur (crème de cassis) into the bottom of the glass, then topping off the drink with a pouring of Champagne. The "royale" refers to the luxury of using Champagne; a simple Kir is an also-delicious mixture of crème de cassis and white wine, instead of the bubbly. There are multiple adaptions, including French Kir and Kir Imperial.

Kir Royale is cookbook author and *For the Culture* magazine publisher Klancy Miller's "go-to hostess cocktail," as she writes in her 2020 book, *Cooking Solo*. "Every hostess and host should know how to make a favorite cocktail for guests. Mine is Kir. . . . When I feel festive, I make it a Kir Royale by substituting Champagne or another sparkling white wine."

Reading her words reminds me of two drinks in Montana mixologist Julian Anderson's early twentieth-century recipe collection: the Vermouth Cocktail, a stirred concoction that blends fruit syrup and orange bitters with Italian vermouth; and the Clover Leaf Cocktail, a gin, raspberry syrup, and lemon juice mixture on which is floated a crown of egg-white foam.

With all three ideas as inspiration, I thoroughly chilled a bottle of dry Chardonnay, then tried using it to top several of my favorite fruit-based liqueurs. Classic crème de cassis ensures that the drink is a little creamy, like Julian's Clover Leaf. But as it turns out, I prefer the clean simplicity of black raspberry–flavored Chambord liqueur best. Homemade Berry Liqueur (page 44) would also be a nice change of pace here. SERVES I

½ ounce (1 tablespoon) **Chambord liqueur** or homemade **Berry Liqueur** (page 44)

6 ounces (1½ cups) well-chilled **Chardonnay wine**

Pour the liqueur into a cocktail glass. Slowly pour the wine over the back side of a bar spoon into the glass. Serve immediately.

SHANDY GAFF

A Shandy is a refreshing drink that layers beer—either porter or ale—with a non-alcoholic beverage. According to *Difford's Guide for Discerning Drinkers*, "The name comes from the London slang for a pint of beer, a shant of gatter" (a *shanty* being a public house, and *gatter* meaning "water").

This British drink was "transplanted with ease" into the colonial Caribbean, Jessica B. Harris explains in her 1991 book, *Sky Juice and Flying Fish: Traditional Caribbean Cooking*.

You can stick with the traditional recipe I offer here, personalizing with any one of today's vast beer selections, from high-proof ales to full-bodied porters with their malty flavor and dark complexions. Or, to maintain continuity with the African Diaspora, you can adopt a Caribbean theme with a light lager from Jamaica, Haiti, Barbados, Belize, the Dominican Republic, or Trinidad and Tobago.

The choice of a non-alcoholic mixer is also up to you. The ginger ale and ale combination is a little sweet and spicy, with a pronounced ginger flavor. If you layer porter with ginger ale, the beer may take over. Ginger beer, which is less sweet, adds brightness to the beers of the Diaspora. And Jamaican cookbook author Enid Donaldson recommends lemonade. SERVES 1

½ cup ginger ale, ginger beer, or lemonade

4 ounces (½ cup) porter, ale, or your choice of beer

Fill an ale glass halfway with the ginger ale. Gradually pour in your choice of porter, ale, or beer. Serve.

SHANDY–GRENADA

Serves 2

1 (12-ounce) bottle light lager beer

1 (12-ounce) bottle ginger beer

2 dashes Angostura

Grating of Nutmeg

Place 2 glass or pewter beer mugs in the freezer to frost. When frosted, mix half a bottle of beer with half a bottle of ginger beer in each mug. Add a splash of bitters and a grating of nutmeg to each mug. Serve immediately and drink chilled.

—Jessica B. Harris, *Sky Juice and Flying Fish: Traditional Caribbean Cooking*, 1991

SHAKEN

Jazz Clubs

JAZZ CLUBS

This Sunday, we been to a Five O'clock Cocktail Sip where they empty
all the different left-over bottles on the bar into the shaker, shake it up,
put in a cherry—and call it a Special.

—*Langston Hughes,*
The Best of Simple, *1961*

T he fictional character Jesse B. Semple is a barfly, soul food connoisseur, and
social observer who, in a collection of sketches Langston Hughes wrote for
the *Chicago Defender,* drops folk wisdom, expresses Black frustrations, and
generally pours out his soul in various bars and nightspots across Harlem during
the Jim Crow era, to a backdrop of jukebox melodies. Hughes nicknamed Semple
"Simple," for holding sway in street language that is sometimes piercing and sometimes garbled. He has been described as an "Everyman for Black Americans."

Simple has interludes with Duke Ellington and Lena Horne, contemplates a
manifesto on greens braised with pork that he calls a "greenology," and knows
whether to bring White Mule (another name for moonshine and bootleg liquor) or
White Horse Scotch Whisky (a brand of blended scotch) to a social affair. In short,
Simple teaches us a little sumpthin' sumpthin' about Black booze and Black clubs
in the years surrounding Prohibition.

Between the end of the Civil War and the Civil Rights era, and despite promises
to end racial discrimination, Southern state and local governments enacted stat-
utes designed to maintain control over African Americans' lives. One of those laws
made it illegal for Black customers to enter establishments that were white owned
or catered to a white clientele. In response, millions of Black folks left the American
South to escape racial violence, pursue economic and educational opportunities,
obtain stability, and create better lives for their families. This mass movement to
Northern, Midwestern, and Western states is known as the Great Migration.

The transplants traveled with shoeboxes containing home-cooked foods like
fried chicken and pound cake, and sought comfort in hospitality businesses where
down-home-style food was sold. Chicken shacks, barbecue joints, and fish-fry

restaurants re-created a sense of home, while bars and music venues soothed souls with spirited drinks and expressive sounds while carrying on cultural music traditions left behind.

One of those traditions was jazz, a rhythmic style of Black music that evolved from a powerful communication tool—performed at funerals, political rallies, and in concerts in New Orleans—into a national phenomenon.

Music districts developed around the new sound in urban centers such as Harlem, Los Angeles, Chicago, and Seattle with clubs like the Cotton Club and the Savoy known for their exceptional house bands, stunningly beautiful chorus lines of Black (albeit usually light-skinned) women dancers in revealing costumes—and a long list of wines, beers, cocktails, and mixed drinks. Still, despite the Black artistry, white gangsters often monopolized this nightlife here, and Black guests were often denied entry unless they were entertainers, kitchen help, or servers. The Cotton Club Girls, a chorus line of "tall, tan, and terrific" dancers, weren't allowed to use the whites-only bathroom, had to pay for their own food and drinks, and were required to come and go through the back door, according to a 1964 article in *The Baltimore Sun*.

It eventually became clear that Blacks needed to have their own place for respectable entertainment. During the height of the Harlem Renaissance, Black folks operated jazz and supper clubs and ballrooms with glamorous atmospheres alongside chicken shacks, rib joints, pool halls, and speakeasies, like the Red Rooster in Harlem.

The chef Marcus Samuelsson's hit Harlem restaurant, Red Rooster, was named after that legendary speakeasy. As he described the original establishment in his *The Red Rooster Cookbook: The Story of Food and Hustle in Harlem*: "It was the place to be. It housed good music and better food and the best cocktails. On Wednesdays, it offered the ultimate culinary high and low: chitterlings and champagne. And unlike Connie's Inn, a nightclub with Black entertainers which catered only to white people, it welcomed all. Blacks, whites, gays, straights, musicians, artists. Even politicians."

Bands left the stage at upscale venues and went to the Black clubs for after-hours entertainment—to eat, drink, and perform the style of music that they wanted to hear. After performing at Harlem's Apollo Theater, for instance, jazz artists walked next door to Showman's Jazz Club, where the bar's "star-maids" (rather than "barmaids") dazzled patrons with their hospitality. Soul food appetizers were free, and it was said that guests celebrating their birthday were served a dinner of chicken and rice and a birthday cake.

In my hometown of Los Angeles, Central Avenue was the heart of the music scene, where jazz developed into its own particular style and small clubs in Watts fought segregation with good music, food, and drink. During World War II, the migrating Black population doubled in Los Angeles, a response to aerospace and defense industry jobs. Restrictive covenants confined nearly 70 percent of them to the area south of downtown, and these "south central" residents depended upon the corridor to provide all of their social needs, historian Steve Isoardi explains in a collection of interviews entitled *The Dark Tree: Jazz and the Community Arts in Los Angeles.*

> During the height of the Harlem Renaissance, Black folks operated jazz and supper clubs and ballrooms with glamorous atmospheres alongside chicken shacks, rib joints, pool halls, and speakeasies.

Ballrooms, theaters, restaurants, and nightclubs that featured all kinds of musical entertainment took hold on Central Avenue. Hot spots included the Elks Ballroom, Dunbar Hotel's Club Alabam, and the Lincoln Theater, sometimes referred to as the West Coast Apollo. After-hours quasi-legal establishments kept the regular club scene going around the clock, members of the Central Avenue Sounds Editorial Committee recalled in *Central Avenue Sounds: Jazz in Los Angeles.* Breakfast clubs, for instance, replicated the breakfast dance at Smalls' Paradise in New York, where the "floor show went on at six o'clock in the morning . . . complete with 25 or 30 people, including the singing waiters and their twirling trays," musician Arnold Shaw explained in his retelling of musicians' inside stories, *The Jazz Age: Popular Music in the 1920s.*

In Houston, the Eldorado Ballroom, situated across the street from Emancipation Park, "was the venue of choice for upscale blues and jazz performances featuring touring stars and local talent, as well as afternoon talent shows and sock-hops," according to a Texas State Historical Association article. Established in 1914 by Anna and Clarence Dupree, the "'Rado" was a prestigious "class venue" that became a symbol of community pride for the Third Ward.

By 1950, however, swanky jazz clubs had mostly vanished. The continuing scourge of Jim Crow segregation, police pressure, landlord disputes, unaffordable rents, evictions, fires, urban renewal, and a shifting entertainment interest from live music to "race records"—portable recordings of music later termed "rhythm & blues"—are among the factors that brought the Black music scenes down.

These days, when I shake up a Cosmo or Lemon Drop Martini, I raise a toast to the Black bartenders of the Jazz Age, an era characterized by exemplary performances and opulent entertaining. I sometimes visualize virtuosos of the bar flipping the shaker forward and back to just chill the beverage inside, with sophisticated nightlife scenes as the backdrop. Other times, I hear the rattling sound of ingredients clanging hard as the mixture is forcefully aerated and whipped together. When this melodious performance is done and the shaker has a nice frosty glow, the libation is strained and poured into a fancy cocktail glass chosen to enhance the drink and amplify its character. Thelonious Monk, Duke Ellington, Louis Armstrong, Dizzy Gillespie, and Ella Fitzgerald come back into play.

I am awash in the spirit of African American culinary innovation—a pleasure that chef, restaurateur, and James Beard Award–winning cookbook author Alexander Smalls fixed to the kitchen in his book *Meals, Music, and Muses: Recipes from My African American Kitchen*, but I have reinterpreted for the bar (the bracketed words are mine):

> *Jazz is made up of three elements: blues, improvisation, and swing. Those are three components that any home cook [or bartender] knows well. . . . Improvisation is a thread that has always been tightly woven into the history of African American cuisine [and cocktails]. The foundations of these recipes were created when they took what they had . . . then cooked [shook and stirred] each dish [and drink] with as much love and finesse as they could summon. Swing . . . is that little extra something that takes it over the top. Swing might come from the butcher [a new spirit] or your favorite grocery store [flavorings and spices] or a farmer's market vendor [seasonal fresh fruits]. . . . Improvisation slides right in when you start remixing.*

ABSINTHE FRAPPÉ

The Old Absinthe House is the oldest bar in New Orleans, and one of the most legendary in America. The part of its history that intrigues me the most, however, involves the African American bartenders who were known and respected for their beverage-making expertise; but unlike the barmen of French and Italian descent, the African American bartenders were left out of the bar's historical records.

According to period advertisements, Old Absinthe House hired Black entertainers like jazz singer Ethel Waters, engaged a Black man named "Uncle Tom" to scare tourists, and posted a listing for an "experienced colored bartender" who could "mix all New Orleans cocktails." And yet, little is known about the bartender ultimately hired for the job, as David Wondrich explains in a 2019 article that chronicled the rebirth of the place.

What is known is that absinthe, the anise-flavored spirit nicknamed the "green fairy," was a darling of the bar before it was outlawed in the United States in 1912 because of the alleged hallucinogenic power of one of its botanical ingredients—wormwood. It returned to markets in 2007 with the same herbaceous green hue and its intense licorice and slightly bitter taste, but with just trace amounts of wormwood. In the intervening years, several absinthe substitutes came to market, including, in the early 1930s, an anise-flavored liqueur called Herbsaint. (Pronounce the name as if it is French—"Urb-san"—and it sounds a lot like *absinthe*.)

Before the absinthe ban, bartenders, including Tom Bullock and Julian Anderson, mastered a technique called "the louche," cloaking the spirit's high alcohol content and mysterious soul power in drinks such as the Absinthe Frappé and the Drip Absinthe Cocktail, which involves using a special absinthe spoon. (When mixed with cold water and ice, absinthe separates, turning cloudy with a milky opaqueness—another great example of the theater of bartending.)

I like this potent drink as an aperitif, and it is featured here to celebrate New Orleans, the birthplace of jazz and the home of a related drink—the Sazerac (page 193)—considered the first American cocktail using Herbsaint.

If you love the taste of black licorice, this dreamy, sweet drink is the one for you. I've added more Benedictine than is customary, which makes for a drink that is sweeter and tastes smoother, while its honey-spice flavor subdues the strong taste of the absinthe's anise. I also like this cocktail made with Curaçao or my own Tangerine Liqueur (page 37); it's a different effect, more citrus than spice.

{recipe continues}

The drink also reminds me of the recipe for anise-seed water published in the first African American book to include recipes for food and home remedies, *The House Servant's Directory*, by Robert Roberts. SERVES 1

½ ounce (1 tablespoon) absinthe

1 tablespoon cold water

2 dashes Angostura bitters

1 teaspoon Benedictine brandy liqueur (or orange liqueur, or homemade Tangerine Liqueur, page 37)

½ cup shaved ice

Combine the absinthe, water, bitters, and Benedictine in a cocktail shaker along with the ice. Close and shake until the outside of the shaker is frosty. (If you don't have a shaker, stir vigorously in a cocktail mixing glass until the mixture becomes cloudy, about 20 seconds.) Strain into a cocktail glass and serve.

A STRONG ANISE-SEED WATER

Take half a pint of the best essential spirits of anise seeds, put this into three quarts of the best brandy, with one quart of boiled water; if not sweet enough, add some clarified sugar, and strain through a jelly bag, this is a most delicious and wholesome water, and a fine stomachic.

—Robert Roberts, *The House Servant's Directory*, 1827

HOW TO MIX ABSINTHE

Mix as follows in a bar or absinthe glass: 1 pony glass of Absinthe, place this into the large glass, which has the shape of a bowl with a small, round hole in the bottom, fill this with finely shaved ice and water; then raise the bowl up high and let the water run or drip into the glass containing the Absinthe; the color of the Absinthe will show when to stop; then pour into the large glass and serve. It will have a milk color and look cloudy.

—Julian Anderson, *Julian's Recipes*, 1919

ORANGE-CHERRY DROP

In his 2009 book, *Vegan Soul Kitchen: Fresh, Healthy, and Creative African-American Cuisine*, chef Bryant Terry adapts the high-octane New Orleans Hurricane by working the juices of California fruit—pomegranate and both navel and blood oranges—into the syrupy-sweet drink of rum, gin, and vodka and serves it in a curvaceous glass. I am not into strolling the streets of the French Quarter in New Orleans sloshed with a potent Hurricane cocktail in hand, but I do love the way Terry's California Slurricane throws to the orange-juice drinks handed down in Black cookbooks through the generations.

In *Miss Williams' Cookery Book,* a 1957 collection by a Nigerian cooking teacher named Miss R. Omosunlola Williams, oranges are peeled and juiced, then the bright orange peel is boiled until the water is imbued with the fruity citrus flavor of the zest. Miss Williams adds the aromatic water to fresh juice and sweetens it to taste. She also makes tonics from pineapple and ginger this way.

In the New World, cooks carried on the orange-tea tradition at Christmastime, as Sallie Ann Robinson recalls in her 2007 cookbook, *Cooking the Gullah Way: Morning, Noon & Night*: "At that time of year Momma would set out oranges and some other fruit in a punch bowl on the dining room table. . . . On occasion we would save the orange peels to boil for a tasty tea, though sneaking a little bit of sugar for the tea wasn't always easy. . . . After boiling the orange peels, we would strain the tea from the peels, which have become soft and juice. Eating the soft peels was fun, too. Making this tea was cheap and easy, and we loved it."

In time, Black cooks built fanciful cocktails on this sweet orange base. There is Southern food expert LaMont Burns's Orange Julep, which tosses some orange juice into a classic Mint Julep; B. Smith's Orange-Cherry Drop, a libation made with vodka, triple sec, and cherry juice; and two drinks that deploy all the theatrics of old-school mixology—the Wedding Ring Cocktail, a showy drink of punched-out orange slices crafted by Bessie M. Gant, the early twentieth-century caterer to the Hollywood stars; and chef-farmer Matthew Raiford's Blood and Sand, a drink made by igniting an orange slice with a match to slightly burn the peel so its oils drip into a combination of scotch, blood orange juice, sweet vermouth, and cherry liqueur.

The following iteration of Bryant Terry's cocktail will transport you to the Big Easy. Plastic Hurricane glass not required. SERVES 2

{recipe continues}

Ice cubes

2 ounces (¼ cup) light rum

2 ounces (¼ cup) dark rum

2 ounces (¼ cup) fresh orange juice

1 ounce (2 tablespoons) fresh tangerine or pineapple juice

1½ tablespoons maraschino cherry juice

1 tablespoon fresh lime juice

1 teaspoon confectioners' sugar

Crushed ice (see page 184)

2 maraschino cherries

2 orange slices

Fill a cocktail shaker two-thirds full with ice. Add the rums, fruit juices, and confectioners' sugar. Close and shake until cold.

Place some crushed ice in two highball glasses. Strain the drink into the glasses, then garnish each with a cherry and an orange slice.

WEDDING RING COCKTAIL

Peel oranges, remove all pulp. slice oranges cross-wise in about ½ inch slices. Cut these slices with a small round cutter into circles. Make a hole in center of each circle (doughnut style). Put rings into cocktail glasses topped with crushed ice. Make a syrup of lime juice, strained honey and gin (do not cook). Pour syrup over orange rings and serve very cold.

—Bessie M Gant, *Bess Gant's Cook Book: Over 600 Original Recipes*, 1947

ORANGE-CHERRY DROP

A SPLENDID SIDECAR

The Sidecar is a classic shake of cognac, orange liqueur, and lemon juice. And here, it is an homage to Southern California's Black citrus growers and ranchers who made new lives for themselves in the early-twentieth-century Inland Empire.

Eliza Tibbets was one of the founders of Riverside, California, and is credited with cultivating the navel orange, a prized foundation of the modern citrus industry. But it was John B. Adams, a Black horticulturist and "budder"—a craftsman who grafts budwood onto existing rootstock to create new trees—who was instrumental in Tibbets's success. And they weren't the only ones. According to research conducted for Sweet N Sour, a public history program presented by the University of California, Riverside, and California State Parks, Black ranchers Israel Beal, David Stokes, and Horace Harroll (who funded a Black newspaper in the area with his fortune) should also be counted among California's citrus pioneers.

To honor them, I looked for orange-based mixed drinks in Black cookbooks and found a wonderful selection, whether the combination involved Cointreau and brandy, Curaçao and gin, or standard orange liqueur with a splash or orange juice and rum. Author Bea Sandler even tossed a little cream into the mix for a drink that tastes like a Dreamsicle—the orange and vanilla ice cream bar of yesterday.

I make the Sidecar supreme with Grand Marnier and VSOP Cognac for a drink befitting the memory of the orange grove owners in my hometown. My Tangerine Liqueur (page 37) is less extravagant but good, too. Serve this Splendid Sidecar in a cocktail glass with a sugared rim. SERVES 1

Sugar

Juice and peel of ½ lemon (about 1½ tablespoons juice)

Ice cubes

1¾ ounces (3½ tablespoons) VSOP Cognac

¾ ounce (1½ tablespoons) Grand Marnier or Tangerine Liqueur (page 37)

Place a few tablespoons of sugar in a dish. Lightly moisten the rim of a cocktail glass with lemon juice, and dip and swirl in the sugar to coat the rim.

Cut a ½-inch-wide strip from the lemon peel, leaving the white pith intact. Set aside.

Fill a cocktail shaker half full with ice. Add the lemon juice, Cognac, and Grand Marnier to the shaker and shake until cold, about 10 seconds. Strain the drink into the sugar-rimmed glass. Squeeze the lemon strip over the drink to express the oils and then discard the peel.

CALIFORNIA SOUL

Here is another tribute to my California roots. This time, the drink celebrates Israel D. Davis of Stockton, the inventor who received patent No. 351,829 for his invention of tonic, a carbonated soft drink flavored with quinine, on November 2, 1886. My recipe takes its cues from the Sherry Punch in Atholene Peyton's *Peytonia Cook Book*, published in 1906. Peyton's simple drink combined California sherry and a sweet-tart base of lemonade. This version adds floral gin and a spicy ginger syrup to a perky mix of lemon and lime. Tonic water adds a slight hint of bitterness and salinity that gives the cocktail balance. SERVES 1

1½ ounces (3 tablespoons) gin

½ ounce (1 tablespoon) dry sherry

1 ounce (2 tablespoons) Ginger Syrup (page 90)

¾ ounce (1½ tablespoons) lemon juice

¾ ounce (1½ tablespoons) fresh lime juice

Ice cubes

4 ounces (½ cup) tonic water

Lemon wheel, for garnish

In a cocktail shaker, combine the gin, sherry, syrup, and lemon and lime juices. Add ice to fill the shaker and shake until cold, about 10 seconds. Fill a Collins glass half full with ice. Pour in the tonic water. Strain the shaken ingredients into the glass, allowing the tonic water to rise to the top and blend. Garnish with the lemon wheel.

COFFEE COCKTAIL

One of the ways old-school bartenders demonstrated their prowess was to prepare a coffee cocktail that was blended without any coffee at all, perhaps in response to wartime food rationing. The Espresso Martini is a modern interpretation of the drink that leans into today's artisanal coffee culture; it involves shaking together equal parts coffee liqueur (usually Kahlúa), vodka, and espresso.

In their 2021 memoir, *Black, White, and The Grey: The Story of an Unexpected Friendship and a Beloved Restaurant*, Mashama Bailey and her partner John O. Morisano contend that their version, The Revolver, which is built on a base of sweet old rye whiskey and luxurious Italian espresso liqueur, is "the best after-dinner cocktail ever created." Maybe so.

But the following iteration, while closely related, is inspired by another cookbook in my collection, from 1988—*Island Cooking: Recipes from the Caribbean*. The author, Dunstan A. Harris, names his drink the Blue Mountain Coffee Cocktail, after Jamaica's highest mountain range and where the famous variety of coffee is grown. Harris turns the spotlight on the distinctive flavor of Tia Maria, Jamaica's coffee liqueur, which is slightly more aromatic than Kahlúa.

I personalized the formula even more, swapping my own Coffee Liqueur and Tangerine Liqueur for the Tia Maria, with its rich coffee notes and hints of citrus and vanilla. In true Martini fashion, the sexy cocktail is garnished with three coffee beans. SERVES I

1½ ounces (3 tablespoons) light rum

¾ ounce (2 teaspoons) vodka

1½ tablespoons homemade Coffee Liqueur (page 28)

1 tablespoon homemade Tangerine Liqueur (page 37)

2 tablespoons fresh orange juice

2 tablespoons fresh lime juice

6 ice cubes

3 coffee beans

In a cocktail shaker, combine the rum, vodka, liqueurs, orange and lime juices, and ice cubes. Shake until cold, about 1 minute. Strain into a Martini glass. Garnish with the coffee beans.

NOTE: Instead of using the homemade liqueurs, you may substitute Tia Maria and increase the orange juice to ¼ cup.

COFFEE COCKTAIL

Fill large Bar glass ⅔ full Shaved Ice.

1 fresh Egg.

1 teaspoonful Bar Sugar.

1 jigger Port Wine.

1 pony Brandy.

Shake; strain into medium thin glass; grate Nutmeg on top and serve.

—Tom Bullock,
The Ideal Bartender, 1917

CLOVER LEAF

The Clover Leaf is a floral, fruity, and sweet gin drink, made with grenadine (pomegranate syrup), lemon juice, and egg whites, resulting in a cocktail with the taste and mouthfeel of berry cream soda. It is sometimes confused with the Clover Club, which uses raspberry syrup in place of the grenadine and vermouth for the lemon juice. (Longtime Tulsa caterer Cleora Butler enjoyed combining grenadine and vermouth—pantry staples that are more accessible than raspberry syrup and fresh lemon juice.) Either way, the drink is sensational, and is another delicious way to serve that homemade grenadine (from page 73) mixed with Old Tom gin, which is mild and smooth.

If you prefer raspberry syrup to the grenadine, this updated option relies on Chambord, a luxury brand of black raspberry liqueur, to tone down some of the sugar. Pasteurized egg whites or half-and-half also replace the frothy raw egg. In either case, this technique demonstrates the high art of cocktail making, shaking to create a beautiful crown of foam. SERVES I

½ ounce (1 tablespoon) Chambord liqueur or Pomegranate Grenadine (page 73)

1 tablespoon fresh lemon juice

2 tablespoons pasteurized egg whites, or 1 tablespoon half-and-half

1 to 1½ ounces (2 to 3 tablespoons) Old Tom gin

Ice cubes

1 fresh mint leaf

Combine the Chambord or grenadine, lemon juice, egg white or half-and-half, and gin in a cocktail shaker with ice cubes. Shake vigorously for 10 seconds, until the ingredients are cold and the mix is frothy with a pink blush. Strain into a Martini or coupe cocktail glass, making sure there is a thin layer of foam and a few small ice chips floating on top. Garnish with the mint leaf.

CLOVER CLUB COCKTAIL

3 parts gin

1 part French vermouth

1 part grenadine

White of 1 egg

Cracked ice

Shake well and serve. Yields 4 cocktails.

—Cleora Butler, *Cleora's Kitchens: The Memoir of a Cook & Eight Decades of Great American Food,* 1985

COSMOPOLITAN

I love playing with the elements of this smooth and slightly pink libation. You may recognize it from the hit television series *Sex and the City*, but serving the cocktail to your guests is also a play on the classic red summertime punches that African American cookbook authors mixed from cranberry juice, citrus, and ginger ale; and for spirited adventures, they used vodka or Champagne in lieu of ginger ale.

Mix budget-friendly Cosmos with average-priced vodka—what bartenders call "the well" or "rail"—triple sec, and up to ¼ cup of sweet-tart cranberry juice (the juice helps inexpensive booze go down easier). Or, make them premium with top-shelf vodka like Belvedere, Cointreau, and less cranberry juice so the flavors of the alcohol shine through. Some folks also rely upon citron vodka for a little sparkle, but I prefer to control the acidity and balance by adding my own lime.

Mixing equal parts vodka and cranberry juice and adding a squirt of lime yields a "clean refresher" that rap legend Snoop Dogg calls the "Happy Hour Vodka Cranberry" in his 2018 cookbook, *From Crook to Cook: Platinum Recipes from Tha Boss Dogg's Kitchen.*

The one must-have glassware amid all the variations is the Martini glass. Snoop serves his Vodka Cranberry cocktail in a rocks glass over ice, but I like the large bowl of the Martini glass, with its svelte stem making you feel sexy when you drink from it. Invest in a good one. SERVES 1

1½ to 2 ounces (3 to 4 tablespoons) vodka

¼ cup fresh lime juice

2 to 4 tablespoons cranberry juice

½ ounce (1 tablespoon) Cointreau orange liqueur, or 1 tablespoon homemade Tangerine Liqueur (page 37)

Ice cubes

1 lime twist

In a cocktail shaker, combine the vodka, lime and cranberry juices, and Cointreau. Fill the shaker with ice and shake vigorously for 20 seconds, until cold. Strain into a chilled Martini glass. Rub the lime twist around the rim of the glass, then drop the twist into the drink to serve.

CUCUMBER COLLINS

The standard Tom Collins combines gin, lemon or lime juice, and carbonated water in a tall, cylindrical glass. The cooling summertime libation is an ideal option for exploring the various flavors that master distillers rely upon to make their gins unique. Sometimes, I like Old Tom gin for its smooth, mild juniper notes, but in this lovely cocktail a more fragrant gin really shows off when combined with lemon juice and the melon-like notes of cucumber.

I could not resist fidgeting with the Cucumber Splash in *Melba's American Comfort* so as to up my Collins game. Melba Wilson is owner of the iconic Harlem restaurant Melba's, and is the creator of a fried chicken recipe that won Bobby Flay's *Throwdown!* competition on his Food Network television program. In her 2021 book, Melba muddles a thick slice of cucumber in the bottom of a cocktail shaker, then adds Hendrick's gin, elderflower liqueur, and lemon juice. The elderflower's floral undertones take the place of sugar or simple syrup; it's a perfect foil for the aromatic gin, which is infused with rose and cucumber. I also love this drink with Maior gin, a delicate Spanish spirit distilled from Mediterranean figs, rosemary, and orange botanicals. For my version, I upped the gin, lemon, and soda for more punch and a more refreshing effervescence. SERVES 1

1 (½-inch-thick) slice of peeled cucumber

2 ounces (¼ cup) gin of choice (preferably Hendrick's or Maior)

1 ounce (2 tablespoons) St-Germain Elderflower liqueur

2 tablespoons fresh lemon juice

Ice cubes

Crushed ice (see page 184)

½ cup lemon-flavored sparkling water

1 lemon twist

1 long, thin strip of cucumber (made with a vegetable peeler)

In a cocktail shaker, muddle the thick cucumber slice until juicy. Add the gin, liqueur, and lemon juice. Fill with ice cubes. Shake hard for 10 seconds to mix well.

Fill a Collins glass halfway with crushed ice. Strain the gin mixture into the glass and top off with the sparkling water. Garnish with the lemon twist and cucumber slice.

GIN FIZZ

Fizzes are made with liquor, citrus juices, and sugar, and are served in a tall glass filled with fizzy carbonated water. A Golden Fizz calls for an egg yolk, while the Ramos Fizz ups that game by adding frothy egg white, heavy cream, and orange flower water for a stunning cocktail that appears to be crowned with meringue.

The Ramos Fizz was once known as the "New Orleans Fizz," and legend tells us that it took nearly two dozen bartenders to complete the required ten minutes or so of shaking, passing the shaker with the mix from one to another. During the Mardi Gras carnival season of 1915, thirty-two staff members were reportedly on site at once, just to shake the drink. The mixing of a Ramos is an entertaining show to watch, but it can be a complex drink to make.

Domestic worker Rebecca West presents three versions of the Gin Fizz in her 1942 recipe collection *Rebecca's Cookbook*. One of them, the Raspberry Fizz, dismisses the egg and instead sports a cheerful red blush from raspberry juice. And in 1990, Queen Ida Guillory simplified the technique by skipping the shaking and instead whirring the classic ingredients in a blender, as presented in her celebration of Louisiana living, *Cookin' with Queen Ida: Bon Temps Creole Recipes (and Stories) from the Queen of Zydeco Music*.

You can shake my version, which focuses on the classic flavors of gin, orange flower water, and milk; add fruit the way West does; or blend the mix with ice cubes for a slushy rendition and serve at brunch, as Guillory suggests. In spite of food safety concerns, I've retained the raw egg white because of its connection to Creole bar-keeping traditions. The citrus and alcohol in the cocktail will help sterilize the egg, but be sure to use a fresh egg white; or if you prefer, feel free to use its equivalent substitute. SERVES I

---

1 tablespoon fresh lemon juice

2 dashes of orange flower water (optional)

1 egg white (or equivalent egg white substitute)

1 teaspoon confectioners' sugar

1 ounce (2 tablespoons) Tanqueray gin

2 tablespoons whole milk or half-and-half

Ice cubes

2 tablespoons sparkling water

In a cocktail shaker, combine the lemon juice, orange flower water (if using), egg white, confectioners' sugar, gin, milk or half-and-half, and ice cubes. Shake vigorously for 30 seconds.

Fill a Collins glass with fresh ice cubes and strain the beverage into the glass. Slowly pour the sparkling water on top, allowing the fizz to slightly rise above the glass rim. Serve with a straw.

RASPBERRY FIZZ

A drink of gin, a teaspoonful of sugar, two tablespoonfuls of raspberry juice and three tablespoonfuls of cream. Shake well with ice, strain into a large glass, and add very cold seltzer.

LONG GIN FIZZ

Muddle half a lemon in a glass with about a tablespoonful of granulated sugar and the juice of half an orange. Add two jiggers of gin and the white of an egg. Shake well until it's thoroughly cold, and strain it into a glass and use the siphon.

NEW ORLEANS
SILVER FIZZ

Muddle half a lime in a glass with three teaspoonfuls of powdered sugar. Put fine ice with it in the shaker. Add two jiggers of brandy, a jigger of cream, six dashes of orange flower water and three dashes of Jamaica rum. Shake thoroughly, and then shake some more. Strain it into a gin fizz glass or goblet, and then use the siphon.

—Rebecca West,
Rebecca's Cookbook, 1942

MAI TAI

The Mai Tai is type of tiki drink made with rum, Curaçao, lemon juice, and orgeat syrup, and shaken with crushed ice. Barmasters have revised the recipe over the years to accommodate changes in rum distilling. Sometimes, grenadine or pineapple juice is added for color and to bring up the sweetness. But the rum is the thing: Shannon Mustipher, cocktail consultant and spirits educator, calls for rhum agricole blanc and an aged demerara rum in her 2019 book, *Tiki: Modern Tropical Cocktails*, but she allows for some personalizing: "Whatever rums you select should display the same grassy, vegetal notes that characterize traditional Jamaican rums."

For an aromatic stand-in for the orgeat syrup in this riff on Mustipher's Mai Tai, consider Amaretto or Frangelico liqueur. SERVES 1

1 ounce (2 tablespoons) white rum
or amber rhum agricole

¾ ounce (1½ tablespoons) Jamaican
dark rum

2 tablespoons fresh lime juice

¾ ounce (1½ tablespoons) homemade
Tangerine Liqueur (page 37)

1 tablespoon orgeat (almond) syrup,
or ½ ounce (1 tablespoon) Amaretto or
Frangelico liqueur

Crushed ice (see page 184)

1 lime twist

1 orange wheel or peeled pineapple quarter

1 maraschino cherry

In a cocktail shaker, combine the rums, lime juice, tangerine liqueur, and orgeat syrup with about ½ cup crushed ice. Shake cold for 20 seconds. Strain into a rocks glass. Squeeze the lime twist over the cocktail and discard. Garnish with the orange wheel or pineapple skewered with a cherry.

SHERRY COBBLER

A Cobbler is a refreshing iced drink made with wine or liquor, fruit, and sugar; it is delightful when the weather is hot. When made with a good sherry, that sweet-tart flavor is balanced by the oaky, nutty taste of the wine.

Tom Bullock offered the Cobbler two ways—one decorated with citrus fruit, the other garnished with a splash of port. Julian Anderson allowed the fresh fruit to do the sweetening work; he simply stirred mineral water into sherry, then decorated the fortified wine with grapes, oranges, pineapple, and berries. Elsewhere, old-school recipes called for a teaspoon of powdered sugar in addition to the fruit syrup; but that taste was too saccharine for me.

I borrowed from them all, giving you some room to make the Cobbler your own. For instance, if fruit flavor is your thing, add pineapple syrup, as Bullock does. If you're not a pineapple fan, a little simple syrup will do. Just don't skimp on the sherry; I like the nutty taste of Amontillado sherry here. SERVES I

1 orange wheel

1 lime wheel

½ tablespoon Pineapple Syrup (page 92) or Simple Syrup (page 31)

2½ ounces (5 tablespoons) Amontillado sherry

Ice cubes

Crushed ice (see page 184)

1 fresh blackberry, for garnish

Place the orange and lime wheels in a cocktail shaker along with the syrup. Muddle until the fruit releases its juices. Add the sherry and ice cubes and shake until cold, about 20 seconds. Fill a sherry glass with crushed ice, then strain the cocktail into the glass. Garnish with the blackberry. Serve with a straw.

CALIFORNIA SHERRY COBBLER

1 pony of Pineapple Syrup in large Bar glass.

2 jiggers California Sherry.

Fill glass with Shaved Ice; stir well; decorate with Fruit; dash a little Port Wine on top and serve with Straws.

—Tom Bullock,
The Ideal Bartender, 1917

SPARKLING WATERMELON LEMONADE

Bartenders Julian Anderson and Tom Bullock punched up the flavor of classic, fresh-squeezed lemonade with a spike of whiskey or a splash of fruit cordial. In recent years, African American cooks have added watermelon to the mix, reclaiming the fruit from its relentless stereotyping.

And that's where this recipe gets its flair. To make a watermelon-infused adaptation of Julian Anderson's Kentucky Lemonade, I distilled my version down to the essentials by reimagining flavoring ingredients in melon-based drinks found in Delta Sigma Theta Sorority's 2004 book, *Occasions to Savor: Our Meals, Menus and Memories*, as well as chef Jerome Grant's Watermelon with Lemon Verbena from the 2018 collection *Sweet Home Café Cookbook*; and Sunny Anderson's Watermelon and Cucumber Lemonade, from her 2013 book, *Sunny's Kitchen*. In my version, the beverage is not really shaken; it gets its smooth finish from a quick whir of the watermelon in the blender.

Make this refreshing cocktail—combining lemonade, watermelon juice, and sparkling wine—to salute the authors named here. And while you're squeezing about half a dozen lemons for the juice, don't forget about John Thomas White, who in 1896 received a patent for an improved lemon squeezer. SERVES 6 TO 8

¾ cup lemon juice

¾ cup granulated sugar

¼ cup finely grated lemon zest, lightly packed

6 cups diced seedless watermelon

Juice of 2 limes

1 (750-ml) bottle chilled prosecco or other sparkling wine

Watermelon wedges (optional)

In a small saucepan, combine the lemon juice and sugar. Bring to a boil over medium heat, stirring until the sugar is dissolved. Reduce the heat to medium-low and simmer for 2 minutes. Remove from the heat and stir in the lemon zest. Cool completely, then strain through a fine-mesh strainer. Transfer the lemon syrup to a jar, cover, and refrigerate several hours, until thoroughly chilled.

Puree the diced melon in a blender until liquefied. (Alternatively, you can mash the melon with a potato masher, but the juice won't be fully extracted.) Strain the melon

{recipe continues}

through a a fine-mesh strainer, pressing gently with the back of a spoon to extract all the juice. Discard the watermelon solids. Refrigerate the juice until thoroughly chilled.

Combine the lemon syrup, lime juice, and watermelon juice in a pitcher and gently stir in the wine. Pour into Collins glasses and serve immediately, each glass garnished with a watermelon slice, if desired.

WATERMELON LEMONADE

Makes 8 servings

½ seedless watermelon, cut into chunks (about 4 cups of chunks)

4 cups water

1½ cups sugar

1 cup bottled lemon juice or juice of 6 lemons

Lemon and watermelon wedges (optional)

Puree watermelon chunks in a blender to get 2½ cups juice. Remove foam (bubbles) from surface of juice and discard. Mix the water, sugar, and lemon juice in a large bowl, stirring until sugar has dissolved. Add the watermelon juice, mixing well. Serve with lemon and watermelon wedges, if desired.

—Delta Sigma Theta Sorority, *Occasions to Savor: Our Meals, Menus and Memories*, 2004

PALOMA

You could say I am wild about Palomas, the sparkling grapefruit-tequila drink from Mexico. While grapefruit juice cocktails don't appear often in Black cookbooks, one known as the Greyhound (grapefruit juice and gin) does show up in *Rebecca's Cookbook*, a 1942 caterer's recipe collection. There also are a couple of grapefruit-based drinks in a more recent addition to my cookbook collection, the 2022 book *Black Mixcellence: A Comprehensive Guide to Black Mixology*, by Tamika Hall and Colin Asare-Appiah.

This contemporary celebration "delivers recipes from modern-day Black & Brown mixologists . . . who are blazing trails," as Asare-Appiah explains in the book's foreword. There are stories that share some of the background I tell in this book, such as the "dark & stormy" history of Caribbean rum, the accomplishments of the Black Mixologists Club, and the lost reputation of Bertie "Birdie" Brown, Montana's moonshine maven. But their approach to their drinks is different.

In *Black Mixcellence*, clever bartenders and mixologists build a cocktail canon upon unique ingredient combinations and fanciful flourishes that turn home mixology into an adventure. They steep their own flavored teas and concoct all sorts of infused liqueurs. They craft simple syrups laced with exotic fruits like lychees, and they beautify simple syrup with herbs and spices such as sage, basil, rosemary, thyme, vanilla, and cinnamon. Their choices seem limitless when it comes to sweet fruit purees—from pears and watermelon to coconut and pineapple. Their garnishes also detour from the ordinary. Expect to find drinks dappled with plenty of froufrou; we're talking edible gold flakes, rose petals, rhubarb ribbons—even popcorn.

My recipe for the Paloma is quite classic, but I love the way black raspberry–flavored Chambord liqueur adds a sweet surprise to the version of a Paloma in *Black Mixcellence*, and you can swap it for the simple syrup called for here. I've been inspired to do that at home on occasion. But I admit I don't source edible gold flakes for my version, as they do. For that, you're on your own! SERVES 1

{recipe continues}

Ice cubes

2 ounces (4 tablespoons) tequila

1 ounce (2 tablespoons) fresh ruby red
grapefruit juice

1 ounce (2 tablespoons) Simple Syrup
(page 31)

½ ounce (1 tablespoon) fresh lime juice

1 ounce (2 tablespoons) grapefruit-flavored
sparkling water

Fill a cocktail shaker halfway with ice. Add
the tequila, grapefruit juice, syrup, and lime
juice. Cover and shake until cold, about
10 seconds.

Strain the drink into a highball glass and
top with the sparkling water.

GREYHOUND

²/₃ drink of dry gin

¹/₃ drink of grapefruit juice

Shake with little ice and serve.

—Rebecca West,
Rebecca's Cookbook, 1942

BEET-A-RITA

A while back, my friend and restaurateur Hoover Alexander concocted a drink he called the Beet-a-Rita to serve alongside a menu of healthy Southern soul food with a Central Texas flair in his Austin restaurant, Hoover's Cooking. His wildly creative take on the margarita got me thinking of the fusion cuisine created by Afro-Mexicans—enslaved people of African descent who sought freedom in Mexico during the 16th and 17th centuries, people whose descendants continue to thrive in Mexico to this day. But that is another story.

Hoover's frozen rita sparked my curiosity. I did some digging through Black recipe books and came across another drink that relies on marinated beet puree for vivid color and unique flavor in Bryant Terry's 2012 cookbook, *The Inspired Vegan: Seasonal Ingredients, Creative Recipes, Mouthwatering Menus*.

Both chefs whip together pureed, cooked beets with citrus juice—Bryant Terry calls for vodka and is inspired by a Bloody Mary aesthetic; Hoover Alexander's play on the frozen margarita whirs the beet puree with gold tequila, triple sec, and ice for a frosty drink that is cool, crisp and veggie forward.

To simplify things, I created a sip that is not as sweet as fruit-based margaritas, and not as vegetal as one might think. I picked up pure bottled beet juice in the health food aisle of the grocery store, swapped in Cointreau for a hint of orange, and sweetened the drink with agave nectar for a clean sweetness sourced from Mexico. It is delicious served frozen or on the rocks. SERVES 2

---

2 ounces (¼ cup) **tequila blanco or reposado**

2 ounces (¼ cup) **Cointreau**

1½ tablespoons lime juice

¼ cup beet juice

2 teaspoons agave or Simple Syrup (page 31)

1 cup ice cubes

Salt

Combine the tequila, Cointreau, lime and beet juices, agave, and ice in a blender. Blend until smooth, 20 to 30 seconds. Serve in a rocks or margarita glass rimmed with salt. Alternatively, mix the drink in a cocktail shaker and strain into a rocks glass over ice.

WHISKEY SOUR

I love Rebecca West's "credit where credit is due" philosophy. In 1942, she included recipes for classic cocktails in her collection, *Rebecca's Cookbook*. Confiding that mixology is not her specialty, she asked friends, including a bartender named Alonzo, to help her concoct the formulas. West was a domestic worker in a journalist's household, so it makes sense she would name names when sourcing her recipes.

The classic Whiskey Sour is made by shaking egg white, lemon juice, simple syrup, and whiskey in a cocktail shaker until the drink is emulsified and topped with foam. But for their sweet-sour base, West and Alonzo mixed sugar and lemon juice in a large ice-filled glass, then topped off the beverage with seltzer.

The use of raw egg in this drink has become optional over time—and I leave it out here. To maintain the drink's tart character, I blur the line between the Alonzo/West version and one by early culinary-school owner Helen Mahammitt, who added orange juice to the mix. Here, orange syrup adds a natural sweetness, while the bitters contribute a nice aroma.

The recipe that follows also appears in the 2021 collection *Black Food: Stories, Art, and Recipes from Across the African Diaspora*, edited by Bryant Terry. SERVES 1

---

2 ounces (4 tablespoons) whiskey

¼ cup fresh orange juice

2 tablespoons fresh lemon juice

1 tablespoon Orange-Flavored Simple Syrup (recipe follows)

2 dashes of Angostura bitters

1 cup ice cubes

1 maraschino cherry

1 orange slice

In a large cocktail shaker, combine the whiskey, orange and lemon juices, simple syrup, bitters, and ice cubes. Close and shake vigorously until the ingredients are well mixed and very cold. Pour the drink into a rocks glass and garnish with a cherry and an orange slice.

ORANGE-FLAVORED SIMPLE SYRUP

MAKES ABOUT ¾ CUP

1 cup water

1 tablespoon grated orange zest

1 cup granulated sugar

In a small heavy-bottomed saucepan, combine the water, orange zest, and sugar. Stir over low heat until the sugar is dissolved. Bring to a boil over medium-high heat, then reduce the heat and simmer until the syrup is reduced by half and is thickened, about 5 minutes.

CHAPTER

6

STIRRED

:::::

Juke Joints

JUKE JOINTS

Much is still hidden about the goings-on in American juke joints, but Alice Walker's description, as fans of Black literature will tell you, is a classic portrayal. I wanted to know about Black booze and bar culture beyond images of juke joints as hotbeds for illicit behavior, prostitution, gambling, dirty dancing, brawling roughnecks, and mason jars filled with bootleg liquor known as white lightning, corn liquor, and moonshine.

But first, some background.

Linguistic scholars root the word *juke* (or *jook*) in a West African word *juga*, meaning "bad or wicked," or the Gullah word *juk,* which means "infamous and disorderly," while other historians believe *juke* is derived from *juice*, a term often used to describe early electric guitars and music players (juice boxes), according to the University of Mississippi's *Mississippi Encyclopedia*.

The concept of a "juke joint" dates to slavery days, when African Americans gathered in the woods to escape the horrors of captivity, for some semblance of life beyond the white planters' gaze. Typically, the amusements involved feasting, dancing, and drinking alcohol to celebrate special events (weddings, funerals, childbirth), or they took place at the end of seasonal community work activities, such as hog killing, corn husking, and log rolling. Sarah Benton, a formerly enslaved woman from Alabama, remembered the simple day-off occasions, often called frolics, this way in a 1936 interview for the Federal Writers' Project: "All us had good dances en frolics on Sadday nights, Mr. Pat Moore used ter watch too, us had ter wurk on Saddays jest de same as eny other day, nother good frolic us had wus on

Xmas and hav parties en dances and my, de times uf dem cornshuckings, nother sech hollering and drinking, as yer ever seed."

In freedom, sharecroppers and farmers socialized in meetups held in wooden "liquor houses," shacks, and barns nestled deep in the backwoods near their farms and in rural towns outside of church communities—"places dominated by Christian values and moralities and somewhat apart from the looser and more secular communities of sharecropper farms and market towns," authors Thad Sitton and James H. Conrad explain in *Freedom Colonies: Independent Black Texans in the Time of Jim Crow.*

While it is true that these unlicensed venues shielded unlawful activities from view during Jim Crow segregation, it is also true that the establishments provided Black working-class people somewhere they could enjoy a few moments of leisure, to eat, drink, and dance. This nuance has left outside observers confused with grossly generalized notions about the types of joints. Sitton and Conrad note that in Houston County for instance, the Vistula community held church-based Saturday night fundraisers with chili and ice cream, whereas wild weekend "balls" at the Murray farm, a few miles to the west, featured live music, dancing, gambling, fighting, and bootleg whiskey. Only the neighboring community members knew the difference between the two.

The juke joint image evolved again with the advent of recorded music that emanated from a box called a "juke box" or "jook box." Interestingly, "Juke" is also the title of a well-known harmonica instrumental recorded by Chicago bluesman Little Walter, which brings to mind the words folklorist and author Zora Neale Hurston wrote in 1934: "Musically speaking, the Jook is the most important place in America."

Black literature, music, and the so-called race films of the mid-twentieth century broaden the contours of Black nightlife during the post–World War II years. Yes, there are characters who drink moonshine from jars and gyrate to dirty dancing music while pistol-packing musicians groan, bleed, and glorify violence. But an alternative theme emerges in films such as *St. Louis Blues, Stormy Weather, Carmen Jones,* and the aptly named *Juke Joints.* Each one sets scenes where talented musicians were paid to play and theaters where exuberant performers bring positive energy to stage shows, from burlesque to musical comedies.

There is dignified singing and dancing. Black bartenders mix drinks behind long L-shaped bars lined with bottles of assorted wines and spirits. Well-dressed couples sit around tables topped with checkered tablecloths and candles, sipping cocktails from glassware, not bottles and jars. Feet pat. Hands clap. Heads bob. Pearl Bailey casually asks a bartender for a Double-Double on the rocks in *Carmen Jones.*

"It was the only place Blacks had to go, to get rid of the blues after a week's hard work in the cotton fields," Kathy Starr, a descendant of sharecroppers, explains in the introduction to *The Soul of Southern Cooking*. Starr learned to cook in her grandmother's café, the Fair Deal, which was located in Hollandale, Mississippi, alongside a "string of little cafés where everybody gathered on the weekends." People ate fried fish, chitterlings, hamburgers, and flatdogs (fried bologna sandwiches). Beer was legal; the hard stuff was not. Starr gives us this peek inside the Fair Deal:

> *If you wanted a half-pint or a pint of whiskey or corn liquor, you could get it at Fair Deal because Grandmama and the chief of police had an "understanding," which was as good as a license to sell. . . . The Seabirds (Seeburg juke boxes) would be jammin' all up and down Blue Front with Howlin' Wolf, Muddy Waters, and B.B. King . . . people danced, ate, drank, and partied 'til the break of day.*

Eventually rural juke joints and cafés like the Fair Deal formalized into storefront business districts across the South. During Jim Crow segregation, these nightclubs, dance halls, juke joints, theaters, clubs, private homes, and some parking lots were thought safe and acceptable places for African American entertainers, including Chubby Checker, James Brown, Ike and Tina Turner, Ray Charles, Jimi Hendrix, and more, to perform. Online sources say Gladys Knight described them like this: "Just a grizzly older man with catfish nuggets, corn fritters, or a pig ear sandwich in a corner." The singer Lou Rawls is credited with popularizing the term "Chitlin' Circuit" for this collection of venues in early interviews, because of its association with chitterlings as "low-class" food.

Integration, changes in the way music was promoted, and upward mobility all but killed the Circuit. Some of the original venues continue to operate. Others are being converted to museums where the traditions of innovation can be preserved. Frederick Douglass Opie, professor of history and foodways at Babson College, summarized the history of the Chitlin Circuit and its influence in an interview for NPR's *Splendid Table*:

> *When we talk about the chitlin' circuit, sometimes there were small hole-in-the-wall places, but the chitlin' circuit also included places like the Apollo Theater in Harlem. Some of these venues were very small, but in urban areas, they could be very large. It's true that you see the term "soul" is so much related to the chitlin' circuit and*

people who made the best they could out of the opportunities they had, whether it'd be spaces to play their music, places to eat food or places to perform when nobody else would have them. It's this whole idea of surviving with dignity amidst a very precarious situation.

In 2002, I hosted the Southern Foodways Alliance's second field trip, called "A Taste of Texas Barbecue," in and around the city of Austin. The weekend kicked off with a Blues and Barbecue Welcome Reception at the Victory Grill, one of the few remaining venues on the circuit. It was a party that "served a bellyful of the best in Austin barbecue and an earful of traditional Texas blues," as we said in the event program. The Victory evolved from its humble beginnings as a ten-cent hamburger stand into a full-service restaurant and club; in its heyday, the Victory served thick-cut pork chops, smothered steaks, and its renowned chili and enchiladas.

So, with *Q's Juke Joint*—Quincy Jones's celebration of juke joint artists—as the soundtrack, I stretched gray duct tape over the original booths to mend the torn and disintegrating red vinyl. We arranged for a team of area pitmasters to serve their barbecue from a buffet positioned near a glass cabinet holding black-and-white photos autographed by performers, and flyers announcing community fundraisers, business meetings, and political campaigns. Local musicians performed and attendees entered the building through the same side door that was once the queue for the nightclub down the stairs.

I stood out front hypnotized by the cracked and yellowing sign hanging above the entrance to the restaurant. It announced the true essence of the place, and the important role the Victory has played in the community for generations. It read: "Nourishing the soul since 1945."

I had constructed the evening to honor the memory of performers who made a way for themselves in a music industry that marginalized them, and I wanted to celebrate the cooks who offered down-home meals that comforted everyone—patrons and performers alike. But at the time I didn't think about the bartenders and the drinks served in plain glassware and mason jars, stirred with a basic long-handled spoon. I hope the libations and stories on the following pages make up for that.

The concept of a "juke joint" dates to slavery days, when African Americans gathered in the woods to escape the horrors of captivity, for some semblance of life beyond the white planters' gaze.

GIN AND JUICE 3.0

"Rolling down the street . . . sippin' on gin and juice" has been a hip-hop anthem ever since Snoop Dogg sang the lyric on his first album, *Doggystyle,* in 1993. Twenty-five years later, the D. O. Double G broke the Guinness World Record for mixing the biggest gin and juice cocktail by stirring up 180 bottles of gin, 154 bottles of apricot brandy, and 38 jugs of orange juice. In 2018, he also published a "laid back" recipe for OG Gin and Juice in a cookbook, *From Crook to Cook: Platinum Recipes from Tha Boss Dogg's Kitchen.* The formula couldn't be simpler: "Take some gin, take some juice, mix it up. That's it."

I traced a similar combination of gin, orange juice, vermouth, and bitters all the way back to Tom Bullock, Julian Anderson, and Rebecca West—the Bronx Cocktail. It resembles a "Perfect Martini," a drink made with half sweet (French) and half dry (Italian) vermouth, and with the addition of the juice. It has come in and out of fashion; *Burke's Complete Cocktail & Drinking Recipes,* published in 1934, called the Bronx Cocktail the third-most famous drink, behind the Martini and the Manhattan.

For a slightly fruit-forward tonic without added sugar, the following Gin and Juice cocktail takes creative cues from West's bartender friend Alonzo, who adds more orange juice than is customary in a Bronx; from the Loafin' Cocktail, which is stirred in LaMont Burns's 1987 book, *Down Home Cooking*; and from Snoop's Remix Gin and Juice, with its ovation to Tanqueray gin. (Snoop also throws in a tropical vibe with the apple-flavored vodka and pineapple juice—"Gin and Juice 2.0," he says.)

Stirring the cocktail dilutes the ice gradually so that it emulsifies with the vermouths. To dilute the alcohol quickly and crown the drink with a thin sheet of ice, shake it. SERVES 1

{recipe continues}

1½ ounces (3 tablespoons) Tanqueray gin

2 tablespoons fresh orange juice

¼ ounce (½ tablespoon) French vermouth

¼ ounce (½ tablespoon) Italian vermouth

Splash of Cointreau or homemade Tangerine Liqueur (page 37; optional)

2 dashes of Angostura or blood orange bitters

Ice cubes

1 orange wheel

Combine the gin, orange juice, vermouths, Cointreau (if using), and bitters in a cocktail mixer with the ice cubes. Stir for 20 seconds, until cold. Rub the rim of a cocktail glass with the orange wheel. Strain the cocktail into the glass and garnish with the orange wheel. Serve immediately.

BRONX, ALONZO

Two parts gin, a half part of vermouth, a tablespoon of orange juice and a dash of Angostura bitters.

—*Rebecca's Cookbook*, Rebecca West, 1942

BITTER CHOCOLATE BOURBON COCKTAIL

When I discovered the early twentieth-century mixed drink called a Chocolate Punch, Chocolate Daisy, or Chocolate Cocktail, the formula reminded me of the time when I asked my bartender son Brandon to help me create a Chocolate Martini to accompany a story about aphrodisiacs that I was writing for *Heart and Soul* magazine.

The Chocolate Cocktail and Chocolate Punch recipes by both Julian Anderson and Tom Bullock shake together an egg, port wine, and liqueur for a rich-bodied drink with subtle hints of chocolate; Julian uses a bit of ground chocolate, while Tom's mix includes no cocoa at all. (I'd guess it gets "chocolate" in its name because of the smooth mouthfeel of the port and shaken egg.) In these old-school recipes, the chocolate flavor seemed too subtle and the herbaceous Chartreuse mostly masked the port.

By midcentury, the chocolate becomes more pronounced with Helen Mahammitt's combination of crème de cacao and cream. And years later, the Darden sisters and caterer Bessie Munson leaned all the way into the chocolate concept in their cookbooks with recipes for a chocolate punch crafted from coffee, homemade hot cocoa, heavy cream, and vanilla ice cream.

All these recipes were drenched in sweetness, with chocolate notes that were almost too bold. The following subtle dessert drink, inspired by T-Pain's Shawty, riffs on them all. The Shawty lives up to its name: short, uber-sweet, and doused in chocolate. I wanted to re-create all that luscious richness but with less sugar; I tried and failed. Cutting the crème de cacao and bitters by half diluted the chocolate punch. So to compromise, I replaced some of the crème de cacao with triple sec, which preserves the chocolate while adding an air of citrus refinement, and I based the whole drink on the rich vanilla and brown-sugar notes of bourbon. SERVES I

{recipe continues}

Ice cubes

1 ounce (2 tablespoons) bourbon

2 ounces (¼ cup) white crème de cacao

¼ ounce (1½ teaspoon) triple sec

1 dash of orange bitters

1 dash of Angostura bitters

2 orange twists

Fill a cocktail mixing glass halfway with ice cubes. Pour in the bourbon, crème de cacao, triple sec, and bitters and stir for 20 seconds. Strain into a chilled highball glass. Carefully twist the orange peel over the drink to express the oils. Serve.

CHOCOLATE PUNCH

Fill large Bar glass ⅔ full Shaved Ice.

1 teaspoonful Bar Sugar.

¼ jigger Curaçao.

1 jigger Port Wine.

1 Egg.

Fill up with milk; shake well; strain into Punch glass; grate Nutmeg on top and serve.

—Tom Bullock,
The Ideal Bartender, 1917

BITTER CHOCOLATE
BOURBON COCKTAIL

HOT BUTTERED RUM

Mention a Hot Toddy, and memories come to mind of high fever, chills, and a cold remedy mix of sugar or honey, whiskey, lemon, and hot water. Saying Hot Buttered Rum, though, takes the mind someplace else entirely. Caribbean and rum recipe books embrace it; I think the soothing drink is a perfect restorative on cold nights.

My formula borrows from Gullah Geechee chef Matthew Raiford's Buttery Scotch and from Tom Bullock's pre-Prohibition drink, Buttered Rum. Raiford stirs together one shot each of scotch or bourbon and adds butterscotch schnapps to capture his passion for hard butterscotch candies. Bullock relies upon real butter for smoothness. The hint of molasses inherent in brown sugar strikes this note in my version. To pump up this toddy as some islanders do, double the rum or substitute spiced rum, and swap apple cider for the water. SERVES I

¾ cup boiling water

1 teaspoon butter

1 teaspoon brown or demerara sugar

⅛ teaspoon vanilla extract

1½ ounces (3 tablespoons) gold or dark rum

Pinch of ground cinnamon

Pinch of grated nutmeg

Fill an Irish Coffee glass with the boiling water. Add the butter, sugar, vanilla, and rum, stirring to mix well. Garnish with the cinnamon and nutmeg. Serve immediately.

BUTTERED RUM

In a Tumbler drop 1 lump of Sugar and dissolve it in a little hot Water, and add:

1¼ jiggers Rum

1 piece of Butter, about the size of a Walnut.

Grate Nutmeg on top and serve.

—Tom Bullock,
The Ideal Bartender, 1917

MANHATTAN

Initially, I thought the austere Manhattan seemed more like a bartender's staple than a soul-stirring beverage that would accommodate the African American sweet tooth. Then, Atholene Peyton's version changed my thinking.

A classic Manhattan is a cocktail in which whiskey is stirred with sweet vermouth, ice cubes, and a dash of bitters, and is garnished with a maraschino cherry. It is light, refreshing, and not too sweet, since there is no added sugar. And it is forgiving. While rye is the classic choice, interpret this cocktail with your favorite whiskey—Canadian, blended, Tennessee whiskey, or bourbon. You can also take inspiration from the variety of mixers that have been stirred into the cocktail over the years, from absinthe and sherry to gomme (gum syrup, made with sugar and gum arabic).

To make it "perfect," stir in half dry and half sweet vermouth. The choice of glassware is also yours—a Manhattan may be strained into a rocks glass or, for an elegant presentation, into a stemmed cocktail glass. A luxurious Luxardo maraschino cherry, as opposed to a generic maraschino, is a must to make this cocktail more complex and "adult," if that fits into your plans.

But back to Atholene Peyton's eye-opening version. In her 1906 recipe collection, *The Peytonia Cook Book*, Peyton, a domestic-science teacher and cooking expert, stipples the time-honored drink with bar syrup, adding a sweetness that makes the drink remarkable. To honor the tradition, I stir in a little bit of the maraschino cherry juice for its bright color and sweet pizzazz. Modern imbibers will marvel. SERVES I

2 ounces (4 tablespoons) rye whiskey

¾ ounce (2 teaspoons) sweet or dry vermouth, or half dry and half sweet

3 dashes of Angostura bitters

½ teaspoon maraschino cherry juice

½ cup ice cubes

1 Luxardo maraschino cherry

In a cocktail mixing glass, combine the whiskey, vermouth, bitters, cherry juice, and ice cubes. Stir cold for 30 seconds. Using a julep strainer, strain the mixture into a rocks or cocktail glass. Garnish with the Luxardo maraschino cherry.

LEMON DROP MARTINI

The Martini is an elegant cocktail, made with gin or vodka and dry vermouth, that will forever be identified with James Bond's iconic bar directive, "Shaken, not stirred." But there are other ways you can personalize this drink.

Nowadays, a Vodka Martini is as popular as the gin-based Martini of yesterday. Some are "dirty," meaning they come with olives, and some are "extra dirty," meaning they come with a splash of olive juice. And while we're at it, let's talk about the olives. The classic olive garnish is one or three olives on a skewer, and they may be stuffed with pimiento, blue cheese, or a jalapeño chile; just be sure the number is odd, not even.

The drink may be served straight up, or be garnished with a simple lemon twist, as Julian Anderson tells us with his Montana Club Cocktail. Or, it can be served with pickled onion, a drink known as a Gibson. In the category of more is best, Tulsa caterer Cleora Butler shakes together all these elements (gin, dry vermouth, and lemon and orange peels with cracked ice), but then she adds a garnish of pickled onion, as is common for a Gibson. Her concoction is called The Old Army Cocktail, and I've included it here to honor her creativity.

When it comes to flavored Martinis, however, the Lemon Drop is my go-to. The recipe that follows is my interpretation of the Lemon Meringue Pie cocktail in the 2011 book *B. Smith Cooks Southern Style* by restaurateur and model Barbara "B." Smith—and it is scrumptious. My mom grows the most sweet-smelling Meyer lemons, so I replaced Smith's citrus vodka with fresh lemon juice; Meyer lemons, if you have them, are less tart and have more of an orange aroma. It may also surprise you to learn that here I prefer the clean ripe-orange taste of triple sec over my homemade Tangerine Liqueur. The tangerine flavor is a little too close to the tropical taste of Curaçao. Or you may use Cointreau, which punches up the alcohol. Smith's hit of limoncello, the Italian digestif, is a fun addition that also channels Butler's over-the-top spirit, but it is optional. SERVES 1

{recipe continues}

2 tablespoons superfine sugar

1 lemon wedge (or reserved peel from squeezing the lemon for juice)

1½ ounces (3 tablespoons) vodka

2 tablespoons fresh Meyer lemon juice

½ ounce (1 tablespoon) triple sec or Cointreau orange liqueur

½ ounce (1 tablespoon) limoncello liqueur (optional)

½ cup ice cubes

1 lemon twist

Fill a saucer with enough of the sugar to coat the rim of a Martini glass. The sugar should be spread slightly wider than your glass and be about ¼ inch deep. Cut a notch in the lemon wedge and rub the lemon around the rim of the glass to dampen it, then invert it into the sugar to coat the rim. Place the glass in the freezer until chilled to the touch.

In a cocktail mixing glass, combine the vodka, lemon juice, triple sec, limoncello (if using), and ice cubes. Stir until cold, about 30 seconds.

Remove the Martini glass from the freezer and strain the cocktail into the glass. Garnish with the lemon twist.

THE OLD ARMY COCKTAIL

2 parts gin

1 part Italian vermouth

Thin zest (peel) of 2 lemons and 1 orange

Cracked ice

Pickled onions

Put in shaker and shake. Pour into glasses of cracked ice and garnish with pickled onion.

—Cleora Butler, *Cleora's Kitchens: The Memoir of a Cook & Eight Decades of Great American Food*, 1985

MINT JULEP

This classic icy drink of fresh mint muddled with sugar and brown spirit is most associated today with Southern gentility, but it has always been a show-stealer for African American mixologists and cookbook authors.

Chef Kevin Mitchell, who has studied the life and work of the formerly enslaved African American chef Nat Fuller, unearthed a review published in 1866 in Georgia's *Daily Constitutionalist* that describes a similar cocktail known as the Brandy Smash, which Fuller created and served on boating excursions in Charleston Harbor: "Nat Fuller, the renowned presiding genius over many a fine dinner and supper, has a cunning way of fixing up water so as to take all the bad taste out of it. We did not get the exact receipt, but believe that ice, brandy, mint and sugar are some of the condiments used."

Nineteenth- and twentieth-century julep recipes ranged from simple syrup–laced concoctions to extravagant preparations made with smashed or whole fruit, or bruised mint leaves. Formerly enslaved cook turned caterer John Dabney, of Richmond, Virginia, was a master of the Hail-Storm Mint Julep, which was ornamented with a fresh fruit topping and, crucially, the newly available miracle of ice, year-round, which Dabney skillfully planed into snow. The city of Richmond honored Dabney with a silver goblet engraved with a thank-you for his "champion juleps." Several newspapers later eulogized him, and his life story is the subject of a 2017 documentary film, *The Hail-Storm: John Dabney in Virginia.*

Other adaptations of the cocktail followed. One that caught my eye includes Atholene Peyton's 1906 elaborate Pineapple Julep, which combines raspberry syrup, gin, Moselle wine, orange juice, maraschino cherry juice, and sliced pineapple, served in a cocktail glass with a garnish of cherries or strawberries. And for her Mint Julep, Peyton bruised mint sprigs with the "best twenty-year-old whisky" and dappled the drink with Jamaican rum.

Today, the wide variety of flavored syrups and spirits on liquor store shelves is inspiring craft cocktail makers to riff on the original. Cookbook author and impresario Bryant Terry freezes the mix and adds an ounce of Crown Royal to give the libation "some Memphis crunk," while chefs Alexander Smalls and JJ Johnson steep bags of black tea in white rum to create their own infused spirit; they shake the ingredients for their Sweet Tea Julep in a jar before pouring it over crushed ice and mint.

{recipe continues}

Feel free to take inspiration from any of these versions. What follows is a classic version. Crushed ice is a must here, as is the straw. SERVES I

5 or 6 mint sprigs

1 teaspoon granulated sugar

2 ounces (4 tablespoons) bourbon or whiskey

Crushed ice (see Note)

Remove the leaves from 4 or 5 mint sprigs; you should have about 10 leaves. Discard the stems and place the leaves in a julep cup along with the sugar. Use a muddler or a wooden spoon to gently mix until the mint releases its oils and the sugar begins to dissolve, about 30 seconds.

Add the bourbon and fill the cup with crushed ice. Stir until the cup becomes chilled and the drink is well mixed, 20 to 30 seconds. Top with additional ice to form a mound above the rim of the cup. Add the remaining mint sprig and serve with a straw.

NOTE: To make crushed ice at home, place 8 to 10 ice cubes in a sturdy cloth or plastic bag and pound with a rubber mallet until finely crushed. Remove and discard any unsightly lumps.

MINT JULEP

Put three sprigs of mint, three half-size sugar dominos and a little water into a glass and muddle them. Fill the glass with fine ice. Add a jigger of whisky and stir well. The ice will melt a little. Add some more, with a half slice of orange. Put another sprig of mint and another jigger of whisky on top, and don't stir. If the glass doesn't frost, then fan it.

—Rebecca West,
Rebecca's Cookbook, 1942

MINT JULEP

PEACH MINT JULEP

Peach Juleps recall a time when nearly every Southern cook stored jars of peach brandy, made from the stone fruit pits, in the root cellar. In his 2022 book *Treme: Stories and Recipes from the Heart of New Orleans*, Lolis Eric Elie gathers tips and recipes for new and interesting twists on classic libations from contemporary bartenders. Elie's Ginger-Peach Julep takes the celebrated mint libation a step further, crafting a fresh-ginger simple syrup to stir into the drink. The recipe also punches up the ginger bite with peppercorns and cloves, which weave in memories of the old Southern-style spiced peaches a friend once brought in a mason jar to welcome us to the Southern Foodways Alliance symposium in Oxford, Mississippi. I love the concept, and as a shortcut, I sometimes muddle the thin slices of a ½-inch piece of fresh ginger along with the mint. The splash of club soda provides some balance.

When fresh peaches are not in season, mix this cocktail with Crown Royal Peach whiskey instead of straight whiskey, or substitute a combination of 1½ ounces (3 tablespoons) straight whiskey and ½ ounce (1 tablespoon) peach brandy. Try the recipe as suggested here, then try it with a tablespoon or two of peach puree for a julep in the Bellini style, imagined by Melba Wilson in her 2021 book, *Melba's American Comfort: 100 Recipes From My Heart to Your Kitchen*. Stir it until the cup appears lightly frosted, as if kissed with drops of early morning dew. SERVES 1

---

4 or 5 mint sprigs

1 ripe peach slice, about ½ inch thick

2 tablespoons Simple Syrup (page 31) or Ginger Syrup (page 90)

2 ounces (4 tablespoons) whiskey

Squeeze of fresh lime (optional)

1 tablespoon club soda or sparkling water (optional)

Crushed ice (see page 184)

Remove the leaves from 3 or 4 of the mint sprigs. Discard the stems and place the leaves in a julep cup along with the peach slice and simple syrup. Use a muddler or wooden spoon to gently muddle until the mint releases its oils and the peach exudes its juice, about 30 seconds depending upon the ripeness of the fruit.

Add the whiskey, then the lime juice and club soda, if using. Fill the cup with the crushed ice. Stir until the cup becomes chilled and the drink is well mixed, about 20 seconds. Top with additional ice to form a mound above the rim of the cup. Garnish with the mint sprig and serve with a straw.

RUM SWIZZLE

A Rum Swizzle is a rum-based cocktail often referred to as "Bermuda's national drink." It will remind you of a Daiquiri with big splashes of orange and pineapple juice, plus the flavored sweetener, falernum liqueur, a spiced lime cordial from Bermuda that tastes of cinnamon and cloves. "The name *swizzle* may be a corruption of 'switchel,' a Caribbean drink made of molasses and water," which is a beverage consumed by the enslaved in the American South and in Brazil, according to Jessica B. Harris, in her 2010 book, *Rum Drinks: 50 Caribbean Cocktails, from Cuba Libre to Rum Daisy.*

Recipes vary, but most say there is one constant: churning the ingredients with a special swizzle stick. That stick is a wooden branch from which protrude several smaller sticks, like the spokes of a wheel. These swizzle sticks can be found in markets throughout the Caribbean and are used as whisks, Harris explains.

The following recipe borrows from two Swizzle recipes. One is Jessica Harris's classic combination of dark Barbadian-style rum (Mount Gay brand), water, and molasses. The other is a syrupy-sweet, potent mix of fruit juice concentrates and high-octane rum, with its intense sweetness coming from rich demerara sugar. The latter recipe appears in the 1994 book *A Traveler's Collection of Black Cooking* by Yvonne M. Jenkins, an Illinois schoolteacher who collected recipes from Liberia, the Caribbean, and the American South. Her version was inspired by her first sips of the drink in Hamilton Parish, Bermuda, she says. For a taste of Bermuda, make this drink with rich-tasting Gosling's Black Seal rum and Mount Gay rum, the latter which will tame the Goslings' dark, spicy notes. SERVES I

Crushed ice (see page 184)

1 ounce (2 tablespoons) gold rum

1 ounce (2 tablespoons) dark rum

1 teaspoon falernum liqueur (or 1 teaspoon demerara sugar and a pinch of ground cinnamon and cloves)

2 tablespoons fresh orange juice

2 tablespoons fresh pineapple juice

½ tablespoon fresh lemon juice

1½ dashes of Angostura bitters

1 orange wheel

1 maraschino cherry

Fill a cocktail mixing glass one-third full with crushed ice. Add the rums, falernum, fruit juices, and bitters. Use a swizzle, a long bar spoon, or a miniature wire whisk to churn or stir for 1 minute, until the mixture is frosty (and the sugar is dissolved, if using).

Fill a Hurricane or Collins glass three-fourths full with fresh crushed ice. Strain the mixture into the glass and garnish with the orange wheel and cherry. Serve with a straw.

SWIZZLE

1 large can pineapple/grapefruit juice (chilled)

1 small can orange juice concentrate

1 small can Hawaiian punch concentrate

6 tablespoons lemon juice

20 ounces Cockspur Rum

10 ounces Gosling's Black Seal Rum

Use a gallon jar or thermos jug. Add the rum slowly to the other ingredients. Fill the jug to the top with ice and swizzle! Serve in cocktail glasses.

—Yvonne M. Jenkins, *A Traveler's Collection of Black Cooking*, 1994

PIÑA COLADA

The Piña Colada—Puerto Rico's national drink—is a creamy, sweet, and fruity cocktail that is a mix of three simple ingredients—rum, coconut cream, and pineapple juice—frappéed with ice in a blender. It tastes like dessert in a glass, and it brings to mind images of white sandy beaches and warm island breezes. Some legacies trace the Piña Colada to a simple rum and coconut water libation that was served over ice with a lime twist and imbibed by natives. The Spanish name translates to "strained pineapple."

Variations—and confusion about the coconut ingredient—abound. Note that coconut water, coconut milk, coconut cream, and cream of coconut are not the same. *Coconut water* is the clear "juice" of the coconut. *Coconut milk* and *coconut cream* are made by cooking the creamy coconut flesh with water, then straining; different degrees of richness and fat content account for the distinction between the two. *Cream of coconut* is a sweetened coconut cream.

I tried this recipe with the bar-staple cream of coconut (the Coco Lopez brand) and found it to be artificially sweet and a little waxy on the tongue. My taste buds were delighted, however, by a combination of coconut cream and coconut milk. This allowed me to manage the sweetness down a bit and to create a drink with natural taste.

Also, you will be surprised at the difference between fresh pineapple that you juice yourself and fresh-cut chunks or canned chunks. For variety, try a good-quality spiced or coconut rum. This recipe also triples easily to serve a crowd.

Several other tips for making Piña Coladas come by way of chef and TV personality Sunny Anderson. For the Easy Piña Colada that is included in her 2013 book, *Sunny's Kitchen: Easy Food for Real Life*, she freezes the coconut cream (I use ice cube trays) and pineapple slices in airtight resealable freezer bags so she can "break off chips" whenever she wants a "mini vacation." She also tops the frosty beverage with additional rum as a finishing touch; ½ ounce (1 tablespoon) is plenty. SERVES I

1½ to 2 ounces (3 to 4 tablespoons) white rum

3 tablespoons coconut cream (or cream of coconut, if you want it sweeter)

1 tablespoon coconut milk (optional)

½ cup chunked fresh pineapple

1½ cups crushed ice (see page 184)

1 fresh pineapple wedge

1 maraschino cherry

{recipe continues}

PIÑA COLADA AND RUM SWIZZLE (PAGE 188)

In a blender, combine 1½ ounces (3 tablespoons) of the rum, the coconut cream, coconut milk (if using), pineapple chunks, and crushed ice. Blend on high speed until smooth and frothy, about 30 seconds. Pour into a Hurricane glass. Carefully pour the remaining ½ ounce (1 tablespoon) rum over the top, if desired. Garnish with a pineapple wedge skewered with a cherry. Serve with a straw.

RUM AND COCONUT WATER

Tradition says this drink is healthful!

1 or more coconuts
2 ounces white rum

Puncture the "eyes" (black spots on the top of coconut). Pour the water from the nut into a glass. (Make sure the coconut milk is not rancid by smelling it.) Strain and serve with rum over ice cubes. Yield: 1 serving.

—Dunstan A. Harris, *Island Cooking: Recipes from the Caribbean*, 1988

SAZERAC

Throughout this book, I have suggested ways you can tweak my recipes to suit your own tastes. Not here. The Sazerac is iconic New Orleans. The aromatic cocktail is made with rye or bourbon, absinthe, and Peychaud's bitters. That's Peychaud's. Period.

Peychaud's bitters is sweeter than Angostura bitters, with a hint of citrus and anise. In some bars, especially outside of New Orleans, Angostura bitters may be used because it is so readily available. Some recipes might even suggest a bit of both bitters. I don't recommend it.

And let's also talk about the absinthe. In my testing of lots of recipes, I decided that this delicate drink needs only enough of the potent herbal liqueur to coat the glass—like oil or butter melted in a pan to keep food from sticking. This allows the flavors of the bitters and rye whiskey to shine. More absinthe will just overpower your drink.

While my recipe is based on the classic, it's worth knowing LaMont Burns's Sazerac recipe, too, because it illustrates the African American spirit of improvisation. Burns, who was a television chef, expert on Southern food, and a restaurateur, published his recipe at a time when absinthe was still outlawed and unavailable. In his 1987 cookbook, *Down Home Southern Cooking*, he suggests a mix of Pernod and anisette, which he punches up with half rum and half whiskey.

Laissez les bontemps rouler! SERVES 1

1½ teaspoons absinthe

1 sugar cube or 1 teaspoon sugar

3 long dashes of Peychaud's bitters (about ¼ teaspoon)

2 ounces (4 tablespoons) rye whiskey

1 lemon peel

Place 1 teaspoon of the absinthe in a rocks glass and roll the glass between your hands, allowing the absinthe to coat the entire inside of the glass. Set aside.

In a cocktail mixing glass, combine the sugar cube and bitters. Use a muddler or wooden spoon to crush the sugar lightly, allowing the bitters to saturate and slowly dissolve the sugar. Add the rye and the remaining ½ teaspoon absinthe. Stir until cold, about 30 seconds.

{recipe continues}

Place a large ice cube in the rocks glass. Using a julep strainer, pour the cocktail mix into the glass. Stir 5 to 10 seconds, allowing the absinthe to blend. Squeeze the lemon peel over the glass to release the oils, then drop the peel in the glass. Serve.

NOTE: A "long dash" of bitters is made by turning the bottle upside down and giving it a hard shake, forcing the bitters to come out more than just a drop, which would happen if the bottle was turned just a 45-degree angle to pour.

SAZERAC

Serves 1

¹/₃ ounce Bacardi rum

¹/₃ ounce rye whisky

¹/₆ ounce anisette

¹/₆ ounce dark rum

1 dash Angostura

1 dash orange bitters

3 dashes Pernod

Put all the ingredients into a cocktail shaker with some cracked ice. Shake well, strain, pour into glass. Serve.

—LaMont Burns,
Down Home Southern Cooking, 1987

POMEGRANATE GIMLET

Gimlets are short drinks made with equal parts gin or vodka and sweetened lime juice; the lime juice typically is a brand called Rose's.

This Pomegranate Gimlet is definitely fancy, with its touch of brandy and grenadine. My recipe modifies Jennifer Booker's from her 2014 cookbook, *Field Peas to Foie Gras: Southern Recipes with a French Accent*. Booker is a Le Cordon Bleu–trained chef who marries the dishes and culinary traditions she experienced growing up on her family's farm in Charleston, Mississippi, with classic French culinary techniques. To replicate the ruby-jewel tones of her homemade pomegranate brandy, I give this high-class cocktail a sweet taste and a pink blush with my Pomegranate Grenadine (page 73). SERVES 1

Crushed ice (see page 184)

2 ounces (4 tablespoons) gin

2 tablespoons fresh lime juice

1 tablespoon Pomegranate Grenadine (page 73)

1 ounce (2 tablespoons) brandy

1 lime wedge

Fill a rocks glass with crushed ice. Add the gin, lime juice, grenadine, and brandy. Stir lightly, then garnish with the lime wedge. Serve.

ZERO PROOF

Resistance

RESISTANCE

Every child rises early on Christmas morning to see the Johnkannaus.
Without them, Christmas would be shorn of its greatest attraction.
They consist of companies of slaves from the plantations . . . two
athletic men, in calico wrappers, have a net thrown over them, covered
with all manner of bright-colored stripes . . . these companies, of a
hundred each, turn out early in the morning, and are allowed to go
round till twelve o'clock, begging for contributions. Not a door is left
unvisited where there is the least chance of obtaining a penny or a glass
of rum. They do not drink while they are out, but carry the rum home in
jugs, to have a carousal.

—**Harriett Jacobs**, Incidents in the
Life of a Slave Girl, *1861*

Long before Dry January was a way to make up for holiday overindulging while also kicking off better health habits for the New Year, African Americans contemplated alcohol consumption. Cooking what you hunted or foraged and drinking alcohol away from the white gaze were tools the enslaved deployed to quietly disrupt a plantation system that ruled over their lives nearly every hour of every day. In the privacy of their cabins or in public gatherings held clandestinely in the woods, bondsmen, as Harriett Jacobs tells us, made a choice: to drink or not to drink.

Jacobs's sentimental autobiography was written the same year the Civil War began, a time when "nearly one-sixth of the total population of the so-called 'land of the free' consisted of slaves." Lydia Maria Child, herself a writer, editor, abolitionist, and author of the cookbook *The Frugal Housewife*, endorsed Jacobs's narrative "with the hope of arousing conscientious and reflecting women at the North to a sense of their duty in the exertion of moral influence on the question of Slavery, on all possible occasions," the introduction to Jacobs's work notes.

Jacobs's dramatic journey unfolds through a series of plantation experiences arranged in themes ranging from the Trials of Girlhood to Christmas Festivities. Her firsthand account of Junkanoo, a masked festival and Christmas tradition in

Jamaica, also known as John Canoe, lifts the veil on a small act of resistance that zero-proofers glorify today: drinking as a choice. It is a thorny story.

To understand this community's refusal to consume alcohol in public, I examined other observations of the period, including *Twelve Years a Slave: Narrative of Solomon Northup* (1853); *Narrative of the Life of Frederick Douglass* (1895); and *What the Slaves Ate: Recollections of African American Foods and Foodways from the Slave Narratives,* by Dwight Eisnach and Herbert C. Covey, a rich analysis of the WPA interviews that were conducted in the late 1930s with formerly enslaved people.

Captives reported that some planters gave out black cake, plum pudding, biscuits, fresh fruit, nuts, candy, "and a big drink on Christmas mornin'." Whiskey, wine, beer, and cherry brandy were mentioned most often. Georgia Baker recalled a chilling element of the festivities: "Merse Alec would call de grown folkses to de big house early in de mornin' and pass 'round a big pewter pitcher full of whiskey, den he would put a little whiskey in dat same pitcher and fill it wid sweetened water and give dat to us chillun. Us called dat 'toddy' or 'dram.'"

While some scholars say a drink of the master's whiskey was a gift that soothed the deprivation of captivity, Douglass believed that slaveholders kept captives drunk to keep control over them. When Jacobs tells us that the men in her community didn't drink the master's liquor until they reached the privacy and safety of their own homes, she is drawing attention to a form of resistance to domination.

For more than a hundred years following Emancipation, some African Americans, in service of racial uplift, persisted in breaking alcohol-swilling stereotypes of Black people. Notions of "respectability" have always been complicated—to whom must we seem "respectable"; at what cost to our freedoms; and in the context of systemic disenfranchisement, what good will it do anyway? But whether their motivation was refusing ceding control of their consciousness and mental faculties, or refusing to be seen as "lazy drunks," there have long been African Americans who refuse alcohol, or choose only to drink behind closed doors.

A'lelia Walker and her mother, the millionaire, self-made beauty product magnate Madam C.J. Walker, purchased two townhouses on West 136th Street in Harlem, New York, in the 1910s. They transformed them into one sprawling residence, which they furnished extravagantly. A'lelia rented out a portion of the townhouse's second floor for wedding receptions, theater company rehearsals, art installations, and fraternity and sorority meetings. But more important, this is where she hosted her "salons," a safe haven where Black artists and thought-leaders gathered to socialize, eat, and drink lavishly despite Jim Crow and the confines of Prohibition.

For more than a hundred years following Emancipation, some African Americans, in service of racial uplift, persisted in breaking alcohol-swilling stereotypes of Black people.

These salons deployed food and hospitality as a tool to resist the social inequities of the era. Guests lounged on plush sofas, noshed on caviar, sipped bootleg Champagne, and enjoyed entertainment provided by queer performers. Frequent guest Langston Hughes described the gatherings this way: "Unless you went early there was no possible way of getting in. Her parties were as crowded as the New York subway at the rush hour."

As the century wore on, Black cookbook authors took a balanced approach to drinking in private spaces and the cocktail hour, featuring recipes for sweet, alcohol-free punches alongside formulas for cocktails and mixed drinks. Atholene Peyton's 1906 cookbook included both types of beverages, and interestingly, Nannie Helen Burroughs, advocate for women's rights, Corresponding Secretary of the Woman's Convention auxiliary to the National Baptist Convention, and Director of the National Training School for Women, penned its foreword. On the other hand, none of the beverages in *The Historical Cookbook of the American Negro,* which was curated in 1948 by the National Council of Negro Women, contained alcohol, not even the recipe for Birthday Toddy. (The NCNW is a Black women's advocacy organization, founded in 1935 by Mary McCleod Bethune. The group published cookbooks through the late 1990s. Alcoholic beverages never made the cut.)

All of these choices brought cookbook author Vertamae Smart-Grosvenor to mind. I first met Vertamae in the early 2000s at a Southern Foodways Alliance symposium in Oxford, Mississippi, and I was moved by the pride she demonstrated as she defended the food and cultural traditions of her people, the Gullah-Geechees of the Carolina Lowcountry. But I hadn't really considered the importance of the gatherings she had hosted in her Upper West Side apartment.

While researching this book, I reread her writings, listened to her NPR radio shows, and revisited her iconic book, *Vibration Cooking: Or, The Travel Notes of a Geechee Girl.*

I learned more about the woman some called a culinary anthropologist, who could be found "holding court"—hosting creatives and performers, and friends of friends, serving a lavish global feast, defending her Gullah-Geechee heritage, and enlarging perceptions of African American culture and cuisine. Through *Vibration Cooking* and her dinner parties—a descendant, I'd say, of the Walkers' salons—she helps us understand the diversity and relevance of African American food and beverage history.

The drinks that follow are spirit-free adaptations of some of the recipes featured throughout this book—the ceremonial libations, tonics, elixirs, teas, punches, and craft cocktails that can make life feel special without leading to stupefying intoxication. Serve them just as you would their liquored-up counterparts—in rocks, highball, or cocktail glasses. If you want to improvise on the time-honored standards, muddle them with fresh fruit and herbs, stir in your own simmered syrups, toss in a little nonalcoholic bubbly. And when you pour these drinks at your next gathering, share the classic Vertamae quip that I started this book with: "I don't drink cocktails and the only one I know how to make is a Molotov, and I'd be a fool to give the recipe here."

HONEY LEMONADE

Lemonade is an African American heritage drink, whether we're talking about the refreshing West African beverage made from steeped lemongrass; the revitalizing fruit waters offered in 1827 by Robert Roberts, the first African American to publish a book on household management; or the sweet-tart hero of today's down-home, summertime menus.

Lemongrass tea, lime tea, and lemonade are among the recipes Dr. Adele Bolden McQueen included in a 1982 cookbook written for culinary students. A home economics professor (and an alumna) at Tuskegee Institute, she ran a test kitchen that focused on "translating food preparation techniques of West Africa to the methods of America, while retaining the essential flavors, textures, and appearance of the original dishes," as she explains in her *West African Cooking for Black American Families*. Lemongrass Herbal Tea also makes an appearance in the National Council of Negro Women's 1998 cookbook *Mother Africa's Table: A Collection of West African and African American Recipes and Cultural Traditions*.

Looking beyond the Motherland, I tried to choose the ideal, Southern-styled lemonade from iconic recipes in my Black cookbook collection, but that was like trying to name a favorite child. Impossible.

To intensify the lemon flavor in a lemonade, Carolyn Quick Tillery, another Tuskegee alumna, macerates lemon slices in hot water, as explained in her 2001 book, *The African-American Heritage Cookbook: Traditional Recipes & Fond Remembrances from Alabama's Renowned Tuskegee Institute*. Meanwhile, Charlotte Jenkins simmers the hulls left over from squeezing lemons in a sugar-water concoction, as described in her 2020 book, *Gullah Cuisine: By Land and By Sea*. Sheila Ferguson pairs sliced lemons and sugar and muddles them with a wooden spoon to capture the vibrant brightness of the peel in her 1994 book, *Soul Food: Classic Cuisine from the Deep South*. This latter technique is also part of the culinary legacy recorded in *The Lost Art of Scratch Cooking: Recipes from the Kitchen of Natha Adkins Parker*, published in 1997; Parker was a beloved domestic worker in Mississippi in the mid-twentieth century. The book is an homage written by her son.

Ultimately, it was Makaila Ulmer's secret formula that came to my rescue, a recipe based not on a technique but on a special ingredient: the complex, floral sweetness of honey. This inspirational young woman founded a lemonade business on her grandmother's honey lemonade recipe after being stung by a bee when she was four years old. In 2015, she appeared on TV's *Shark Tank*, where she received a $60,000 investment for her growing business. I asked Ulmer why anyone would purchase her Me & The Bees Lemonade rather than one of the many established brands on supermarket shelves. Her reply was confident and matter of fact: "Because I'm ten years old."

With that, I returned to the old-fashioned lemonade recipes of the past to extract the most flavor from the fruit, and I swapped in local honey, creating a sweet, cool drink that borrows from everybody. SERVES 6 TO 8

8 small or 4 large lemons

⅓ to ⅔ cup honey

3 cups hot water

1 quart cold water

Ice cubes

Cut 1 lemon into thin slices. Juice the remaining lemons and set the juice aside. Place half the lemon slices in a large pitcher and cover with the honey. Add the lemon juice and pour in the hot water. Do not stir; let cool to room temperature. Stir in the cold water. Refrigerate for several hours until completely chilled. Serve in glasses over ice cubes and garnished with the reserved lemon slices.

OLD-FASHIONED LEMONADE

4 lemons

¾ cup sugar

4 cups cold water

1. Cut lemon in thin slices.

2. Remove seeds.

3. Place slices in bowl, add sugar.

4. Let stand for 10 minutes.

5. Press lemon slices with back of spoon to extract juice.

6. Add cold water.

7. Press lemon slices again.

8. Remove slices, strain mixture and serve over ice.

This is real lemonade.

—Curtis Parker, The Lost Art of Scratch Cooking: Recipes from the Kitchen of Natha Adkins Parker, 1997

"SO-GOOD" RED LEMONADE

Red-hued lemonade isn't just a creative spin on a cool summer drink. It is also one of the dazzling number of recipes for blushing berry lemonades I discovered in classic African American cookbooks. And George Washington Carver, quoted in *The African-American Heritage Cookbook: Traditional Recipes & Fond Memories from Alabama's Renowned Tuskegee Institute*, by Carolyn Quick Tillery, noted the beverage is a menu tradition that goes way back: "[And] the barbecued oxen and hogs and sheep were washed down with gallons of . . . red lemonade."

On Juneteenth, drinking red soda water, red soda pop, or strawberry or raspberry lemonade was a tradition—as customary as eating barbecue and reading General Gordon Granger's General Order No. 3, the proclamation that informed the enslaved in Texas of their freedom. Author Anna Pearl Barrett, in her 1999 young-adult book, *Juneteenth: Celebrating Freedom in Texas*, also tells us that children attending the Emancipation Day celebration in Texas had a unique name for the beverage: it was called "so'good."

In *Jubilee: Recipes from Two Centuries of African American Cooking*, I trace the red drink's lineage from beverages made in Africa with red kola nuts to the molasses water refreshers and berry-flavored waters created by the enslaved in America, to the red soda pop, red punches, and powdered drink mixes of our modern day. Enjoying a chilled red beverage on the June 19 holiday throws to all of these.

For a fun project, contemporary food writer Nicole A. Taylor's 2022 Juneteenth-themed cookbook, *Watermelon and Red Birds*, invites us to try a new, homemade twist on the classic red drink mix, Kool-Aid. Her recipe, inspired by Philadelphia chef Omar Tate, calls for a sugar-sweetened powder you make yourself from freeze-dried strawberries.

For the following recipe, simply mash tender fresh raspberries or puree fresh strawberries in a blender with sugar to create a fruity red base for a lemonade fit for Freedom Day. SERVES 6

2½ cups fresh raspberries or hulled strawberries

1½ cups granulated sugar

5 cups water

1 cup fresh lemon juice (from about 8 small or 4 large lemons)

Ice cubes

Fresh mint sprigs and lemon slices

If using raspberries, combine 1 cup of them and all the sugar in a medium bowl. Mash with a potato masher until the berries soften and the sugar is starting to dissolve, about 1 minute. Stir in another cup of the berries and continue mashing until the sugar is completely dissolved and the berries are juicy. If using strawberries, puree them with the sugar in a blender until smooth, then transfer to a medium bowl.

Stir the water into the berry puree and mix well. Strain the mixture through a fine-mesh sieve into a pitcher, pressing the fruit puree with the back of a spoon to extract as much juice as possible. Stir the lemon juice into the berry mixture. Serve in glasses over ice cubes, and garnish with the remaining whole raspberries and with the mint sprigs and lemon slices.

STRAWBERRY LEMONADE

Makes 1¼ cups powdered mix, for 8 cups lemonade

½ cup (12g) freeze-dried strawberries

1 cup sugar

1 tablespoon citric acid

¼ teaspoon kosher salt

6 lemons

1 cup fresh strawberries

Ice, to serve

Combine the freeze-dried strawberries and sugar in a mini food processor and blend until they become a fine powder. Transfer to an airtight container, add the citric acid and salt, and stir to combine. (The strawberry powder can be stored in the airtight container at room temperature for up to 1 month.)

Juice half the lemons and slice the remaining lemons into thin wheels. Set aside.

To make a large batch of lemonade, combine all the strawberry powder with 8 cups water and the lemon juice in a large pitcher. Stir using a wooden spoon until the sugar has dissolved completely. Add more water to taste, aiming for the lemonade to be on the sweeter side (the ice will dilute it slightly). Strain the lemonade through a fine-mesh sieve, if necessary, and chill until ready to serve. To serve, add the lemon slices and fresh strawberries to the pitcher and top it off with ice.

For an individual serving of lemonade, mix 2 tablespoons of the strawberry powder, 1 cup water, 2 tablespoons lemon juice in a tall glass. Stir with a spoon until the sugar has dissolved. Add ice and garnish with lemon slices and a couple of fresh strawberries.

—Nicole Taylor,
Watermelon and Red Birds, 2022

HOMEMADE LEMONADE

Both iconic cooks Edna Lewis and Vertamae Smart-Grosvenor believed that the purity of the water determined the best lemonade.

Vertamae Smart-Grosvenor's Aunt Virter would go out into nature for the secret to her lemonade: "She would make lemonade with spring water and fresh juicy lemons. I tried it with bottled water and it wasn't as good as hers, but better than with tap water," Grosvenor confides in her 2011 book, *Vibration Cooking: Or, The Traveling Notes of a Geechee Girl.*

The recipe in Lewis's landmark cookbook of refined Black Southern food, *The Taste of Country Cooking*, published in 1976, calls for well water, but she was a little more forgiving, advising, "If you don't have a well, use bottled spring water."

While these cooks were blessed with access to the freshest ingredients, sometimes our pantry items could use a little flavor boost. That's where this recipe comes in. It taps into both my taste memories of the fresh California citrus my mom grew in our backyard and a new recipe for me, found in the 2000 book *The New Low-Country Cooking: 125 Recipes for Coastal Southern Cooking with Innovative Style,* by chef Marvin Woods. Woods, who earned fame as executive chef at Café Beulah in New York City, dapples his lemonade lineup with orange and lime juices. This softens the tartness of the lemon so you can use less sugar than expected, and it gives the drink a more complex, rounder flavor.

Try the following recipe as it is, then adjust the amounts of citrus and sugar to your own taste. If tangerine, grapefruit, or blood orange tickles your fancy, you may want to try it, too. MAKES ABOUT 2½ QUARTS

---

2 quarts water

1½ cups fresh lemon juice

Juice of 1 orange

Juice of 1 lime

1 cup granulated sugar

Ice cubes

In a large pitcher, combine the water, citrus juices, and sugar. Stir vigorously until the sugar is dissolved. Refrigerate, covered, for several hours, until thoroughly chilled. Serve in chilled glasses over ice cubes.

BUBBLY COCKTAIL

If you love bubbles as much as I do, you're probably thinking there would have to be a pretty darn good reason to choose a spirit-free Champagne over the real thing. This recipe is it.

Long before the beverage industry started making alcohol-free spirits, Black caterers and cooks invented recipes for a mock champagne, a diabetic champagne, and an imitation champagne to ensure that guests who didn't imbibe could enjoy festive occasions too.

The combinations are endless. White grape juice or apple juice are favorite bases, and frozen juice concentrates, whether orange, lemon, or grapefruit, add variety. For the bubbles, ginger ale or lemon-lime soda pack additional sweetness, while sparkling water yields lighter and more refreshing drinks.

Eliza's Cook Book: Favorite Recipes Compiled by Negro Culinary Club of Los Angeles is a rare and sophisticated collection by Beatrice Hightower Cates that was published in 1936. It is one of my favorite cookbooks in my library because of the upscale recipes for ladies' luncheon fare, all contributed by club members. A sweet lemon-lime-grapefruit cocktail is among the standouts.

I have also been known to fangirl Lucille Bishop Smith and her 1941 recipe collection, *Lucille's Treasure Chest of Fine Foods*, where the recipe titles are as imaginative as her culinary formulas—from Lemon Glow Punch to Mock Champagne. There is so much to respect about Smith. She was a renowned chef, dietitian, caterer, and inventor of the first packaged mix for making fresh hot rolls.

My spirit-free bubbly recipe that follows reflects the best of both of these two very special cookbooks. I lightened the sweetness of a classic punch-bowl recipe by omitting the sugar that went into the juice base. I also found that for more modern tastes, the subtle flavors in the grape–apple juice base pairs nicely with ginger ale's peppery bite, while the more muted sweetness of the lemon-lime soda allows the pineapple-apple combination to shine. Freezing the mix until slushy is a pro move that will satisfy the frozen cocktail fans at your next party. SERVES 2

{recipe continues}

1 cup white grape or pineapple juice

¼ cup apple juice

¼ cup fresh lemon juice

½ cup lemon-lime soda or ginger ale, chilled

2 small mint sprigs

2 lemon or lime wheels

Combine the juices in a medium pitcher. Stir to mix well. Freeze until slushy, at least 4 hours, stirring occasionally to prevent the mixture from freezing solid.

Spoon the slushy mixture into 2 stemmed cocktail or Champagne glasses. Top with the cold soda. Do not stir or add ice. Garnish each with a mint sprig and a lemon or lime wheel.

MOCK CHAMPAGNE

Here is a Beverage for your "Teen-Age" Parties.

Church groups, Educators, College students, Waldemar Consulars, and Campers have stamped their approval on this Mock Champagne as being the answer to a present need. Here it is:

Put into a punch bowl, cubes of ice, or a molded block of ice or frozen SPRITE. Add a pink rose when semi-frozen.

Mix equal amounts of SPRITE & APPLE JUICE and pour over the ice. Allow it to stand for a few minutes. Serve cold and delight your guests.

Try adding a bit of pink coloring to the Champagne before pouring over the ice, for pink Champagne.

Note: Mix as served to retain the sparkle and zest.

—Lucille Bishop Smith, *Lucille's Treasure Chest of Fine Foods*, 1941

BUBBLY COCKTAIL

COSMOCKPOLITAN

When I encountered the long list of cranberry-orange punches in African American cookbooks, I couldn't help but see a nod to the popular womanish drink, the Cosmopolitan. So, I set out to create a refreshing punch that relies upon cranberry juice for red color and sweet-tart taste, uses orange juice as a stand-in for citrusy orange liqueur, and includes ginger ale, which adds sweetness and ensures the drink tastes perky and festive. I took my cues from recipes in three books: the Cranberry Orange Drink in the *East Austin Garden Club Cookbook* (1990), the Ruby Fruit Punch in *Food for My Household: Recipes by Members of Ebenezer Baptist Church* (1986), and the Cranberry Punch in *Colorful Louisiana Cooking in Black and White* (1988).

The third book is a celebration of Louisiana culinary traditions shared by both African American and white households, Ethel Dixon and Bibby Tate's *Colorful Louisiana Cuisine in Black and White*. In this 1990 cultural celebration, two Louisianians—one a descendant of slaves and the other whose kin once enslaved African Americans on their plantation—each provide recipes for the cookbook. To identify their heritage and style, Dixon marks her recipes with a "B," while Tate's are tagged with a "W." The punch recipe that featured the unique addition of canned cranberry sauce was marked with "B," conveying the spirit of culinary improvisation that has defined soul food—and cooking with soul. SERVES 5

3 cups cranberry juice

½ cup pineapple juice

1 cup fresh orange juice

Juice of 1 lime

1⅓ cups ginger ale

5 orange twists

Combine the juices in a large pitcher. Cover and refrigerate for several hours, until thoroughly chilled. Stir in the ginger ale. Serve in Martini glasses, garnished with the orange twists.

CRANBERRY PUNCH

Serves 150

2 (12 oz) cans frozen lemonade

1 lg can pineapple juice

4 cans cranberry sauce, whipped

4 fifths ginger ale

2 (16 oz) cans frozen orange juice

3½ bottles cranberry cocktail

—Ethel Dixon and Bibby Tate,
*Colorful Louisiana Cooking in
Black and White*, 1988

GINGER CUP

Ginger tea. Ginger punch. Ginger-ade. Ginger ale. Yes, there are some delicious ways with ginger in the African American beverage canon. Formulas for steeping the peppery rhizome in hot water and taming its bite with a splash of lime and taste of honey trace back to West Africa, where fermented ginger beer is a menu constant.

In the United States, recipe writers have valued ginger drinks for good health ever since *The House Servants Directory* by butler Robert Roberts explained the method in 1827: "To make the best ginger beer."

Fast-forward, and there are dozens more riffs on the ginger-drink theme in our history. Food editor Freda DeKnight mixes fresh ginger with orange and lemon juices, and gives it some pizazz with sparkling water in her 1948 cookbook *A Date with a Dish*. Television chef Carla Hall steeps a spiced and spicy habanero-ginger tea that she tops off simply with sparkling water or adds to spirited cocktails, in her 2018 tribute to African American heritage cooking, *Carla Hall's Soul Food: Everyday and Celebration*. And James Beard Award–winning author Hawa Hassan builds an "assertive base" for a potent elixir she calls Ginger Spritz in her 2020 cookbook, *In Bibi's Kitchen: The Recipes and Stories of Grandmothers from the Eight African Countries that Touch the Indian Ocean*, by blitzing ginger, honey, and lemon in the blender. Seltzer or sparkling wine makes the drink sparkle.

Hassan's idea for a fresh ginger drink is a good one, but I choose to stick with a classic approach for this invigorating drink. It starts with a strong ginger-tea base that doubles the amount of fresh ginger found in most formulas. Grating the ginger is often prescribed, but a fine chop is sufficient to release the essential oils. A brief simmer in water that's been laced with lime tames the ginger flavor a bit. And for natural sweeteners I choose pineapple, orange, and lime juices, along with honey in modest measure. I top it all off with sparkling water in a 1:1 ratio. For a perky punch, though, go with 2:1. And for a spirited cocktail, see the Ginger Sunrise on page 105. SERVES 4

{recipe continues}

2 cups Chile Pepper–Ginger Tea (recipe follows)

2 tablespoons fresh orange juice

2 tablespoons pineapple juice

3 tablespoons honey, or to taste

Ice cubes

Sparkling water, as needed

4 orange or lime wheels

4 mint sprigs

In a medium pitcher, combine the Chile Pepper–Ginger Tea, orange and pineapple juices, and honey. Stir well to blend. Cover and refrigerate until thoroughly chilled, at least 4 hours.

To serve, fill four tall glasses halfway with the ice. Pour in ½ cup of the mixture. Top each with sparkling water to achieve desired sweetness (¼ cup for sweet, 1 cup for a mild-tasting punch). Garnish each glass with an orange or lime wheel and add a mint sprig.

CHILE PEPPER–GINGER TEA

MAKES ABOUT 2 CUPS

2 cups water

½ cup peeled and finely chopped fresh ginger

1 tablespoon coarsely chopped jalapeño chile (you may use a hotter pepper if desired)

Grated zest and juice of 1 lime (about 2 tablespoons juice)

In a small saucepan, combine the water, ginger, chile, and lime zest and juice. Bring to a boil over high heat, then reduce the heat to medium-low and simmer for 10 minutes. Remove from the heat and let cool completely.

Use a fine-mesh sieve to strain the liquid. Pour the liquid into a glass pint jar, cover, and refrigerate for up to 1 month.

SWEET ORANGE COCKTAIL

While researching classic combinations for this book, I was surprised by the number of orange drink recipes in Black cookbooks—formulas that could be traced directly from Africa to the American South, and today they seem especially awe-inspiring.

The recipe journey begins with *Miss Williams' Cookery Book*, a treasure trove of Nigerian recipes published in 1957. Here, her Orange Drink is made by pouring boiling water on the thin rind of an orange after it has been juiced; this is done to extract the oils from the flavorful sweet essence known to cooks as the zest. The resulting delicate water is then added to orange juice and sweetened as desired—it's essentially an orange-enriched orange juice.

Next, Sallie Ann Robinson, a Gullah chef who was born and raised on Daufuskie Island, one of South Carolina's barrier islands, recalls a similar tradition in her 2007 book, *Cooking the Gullah Way: Morning, Noon, & Night.* The Gullahs are descendants of enslaved people, and they have maintained many African food and other cultural traditions. Robinson remembers an orange "tea" she enjoyed as a child during Christmastime; she describes it this way: "On occasion we would save the orange peels to boil for a tasty tea, though sneaking a little bit of sugar for the tea wasn't easy. . . . After boiling the orange peels, we would strain the tea from the peels, which would have become soft and juicy. Eating the soft peels was fun, too. Making this tea was cheap and easy, and we loved it."

Steeping orange peel in hot simple syrup is another technique Black cooks have trusted to draw extra flavor from fruit. A recipe for it comes to us by way of *The Chef,* a recipe collection produced in 1944 by the City Federation of Colored Women's Clubs. The clubwomen gathered recipes to raise funds for the Girl's Receiving Home, a house designed to protect "neglected, abandoned or delinquent" girls from street life or jail. Their combination of flavors reminded me of orangeade or the citrus coolers that were a hallmark of hot summer afternoons when I was a child.

For my version that follows here, I embraced a bit of all these recipes, but wanted to create an orange drink with dynamic taste and vivid color. I started with Cara Cara and blood oranges, and I mixed them with less sugar than many recipes call for. (I love the tangy hint of grapefruit in these varieties, and I wanted a drink that tasted more of citrus than of sugar.) Fresh-squeezed navel oranges work well too, so feel free to try orange combinations that suit your own tastes. Just don't be tempted to add the peel to the syrup while it cooks; it will taste slightly scorched. SERVES 4

{recipe continues}

½ cup water

½ cup granulated sugar

Juice and grated zest of 2 large oranges (about 1 cup)

1 cup fresh lemon juice

Crushed ice (see page 184)

2 cups sparkling water, or as needed

4 orange wheels

Mint sprigs

In a medium saucepan, combine the water and sugar. Bring it to a boil over medium heat, then reduce the heat to low and simmer for 10 minutes, until the syrup has reduced a bit. Remove from the heat and add the orange zest. Let stand, covered, to allow the flavors to blend, at least 1 hour.

Strain the syrup through a fine-mesh sieve into a medium pitcher, pressing out the last bits of syrup from the pulp with a spoon. Discard the orange zest. Add the orange and lemon juices to the pitcher, cover, and refrigerate several hours to chill thoroughly.

To serve, fill tall glasses with crushed ice and pour in about ⅓ cup of the juice mixture. Fill the glasses with sparkling water. Garnish with the orange wheels and mint.

ORANGE DRINK

1 orange

½ pint cold water

Sugar to taste

1. Squeeze out juice.

2. Add sugar and water.

3. Peel the orange very thinly.

4. Pour ½ pint of boiling water on the thin rind, and cover.

5. Leave until cool, by which time the flavour of the peel will be imparted to the water.

6. Add the flavoured water to the orange juice.

7. Sweeten to taste.

— R. Omosunlola Williams,
Miss Williams' Cookery Book, 1957

LIME-MINT SPARKLER

The National Council of Negro Women (NCNW) turned Black culinary pride into a cause for celebration in their 1958 crowd-sourced recipe collection, *The Historical Cookbook of the American Negro: The Classic Yearlong Celebration of Black Heritage from Emancipation Proclamation Breakfast Cake to Wandering Pilgrim's Stew.* "[The Council] took charge of their cultural heritage and incorporated into it a global, inclusive philosophy that promoted diversity and democracy," Professor Anne L. Bower writes in the introduction to the 2000 reprinted edition.

The NCNW went on to publish four more recipe books centered on Black history and culinary traditions. One of them, *Mother Africa's Table: A Collection of West African and African American Recipes and Cultural Traditions* (1998), features a full section on beverages, such as tropical fruit-, herb-, and nut-flavored and non-alcoholic drinks, spiced tea, West African fruit punch, a watermelon ginger refresher, and ginger beer.

I updated the following alcohol-free homage to the Mint Julep from the Lime and Ginger Drink, included in the Indianapolis Section of NCNW's *Favorite Recipes from Our Best Cooks* (1982). It features a homemade lime-scented mint infusion that you use to flavor ginger ale; for this, choose your favorite ginger ale, from syrupy to spicy—they will all work. And for a drink that resembles the classic Mint Julep, I doubled the amount of mint in the NCNW recipe and replaced some of the sugar with soda. SERVES 2

---

1 lime

1 tablespoon granulated sugar

¼ cup chopped fresh mint

¾ cup boiling water

2 cups lemon-lime soda or ginger ale

Crushed ice (see page 184)

2 mint sprigs

Using a vegetable peeler, carefully peel the lime without removing any of the white pith. Cut the lime in half and squeeze the juice from one half. Reserve the remaining lime half for another use. In a cocktail glass, combine the lime zest and juice, the sugar, mint, and boiling water. Cool to room temperature, stirring occasionally to extract the flavors from the lime and mint. Cover and refrigerate several hours, until cold.

Strain the mixture through a fine-mesh sieve into a small pitcher. Stir in the soda. Fill two julep cups halfway with crushed ice. Pour the lime mixture into the cups. Top with additional ice, mounding it above the rim. Garnish each with a mint sprig and serve with a straw.

BERRY-SPICED TEA

Edna Lewis was an iced-tea champion. Tea bags? She was not so much a champion of those.

The "Grande Dame of Southern Cooking," known and respected for writing cookbooks that capture the farm-fresh, seasonal cooking of her formerly enslaved Virginia family, insists in her 1976 book, *The Taste of Country Cooking,* that the best iced tea is brewed with good-quality orange pekoe or a blend of green tea leaves. It should be made from pure spring or well water, steeped only 7 to 8 minutes, and strained while still hot through a stainless-steel strainer over a 1-quart chunk of ice. "This will prevent the tea from becoming cloudy before being served," she says, demonstrating the refined attention to detail that she was raised with.

I prefer loose tea leaves over tea bags, too. But I have found that adding fruit to tea brewed from bags is just fine when a tea punch is on the menu. The idea has been around as long as African American caterers and hostesses have blended fruit and tea to quench their thirsty crowds.

Mid-twentieth-century caterers Lucille Bishop Smith and Jessie Payne start their iced tea punch with steeped orange pekoe, adding orange and lemon juice, plus pineapple or grapefruit juice, and a generous pour of ginger ale for fizzy sweet flavor. Smith served hers hot; "Paynie," as she was known and loved in Lexington, North Carolina, where she operated a catering business for prominent families and club women, served hers cold. (Her menus and recipes were tested and published in 1955, in a keepsake cookbook entitled *Paynie's Parties.*)

Several cookbook authors writing during the soul food era of the 1960s and '70s took an unconventional approach to perking up the flavor of ordinary tea with fruit. One diluted flavored gelatin in the base of hot tea to give the finished drink some character. Another peppered their tea punch with cinnamon and cloves for a warm winter vibe. For a cool, less sweet alternative to lemonade, using berries adds a vivid color that turns citrus-laced or spiced tea into warm-weather thirst-quenchers.

My infusion here is an adaptation of the Blueberry Sweet Tea found in contemporary Atlanta chef Todd Richards's 2018 book *Soul: A Chef's Culinary Evolution in 150 Recipes.* The cookbook looks back through generations to present a lovely "homage to the cuisine of my family and ancestors," as he says. His summertime beverage is a tribute to the sweet tea his aunt brewed in a jar, using the hot sun outside her Hot Springs, Arkansas, home. "It seemed like there was a sort of purity in tea brewed this way," Richards notes.

{recipe continues}

I swapped blackberries for his blueberries, and opted for classic spices—cloves and cinnamon—instead of the star anise and black peppercorns in his prescription. I also popped handmade party ice cubes into my version, another trick I picked up from the old-time tea makers. And the lemon juice gives the tea some zing.

Of all the recipes I tested for a spiced or fruit tea, this one drew me right back to Edna Lewis's kitchen and her Southern cooking wisdom. It is vibrant and delicious all year round. (Try it with cranberries during the winter holidays.) All that is missing is the porch swing. SERVES 8

2 quarts water

12 standard-size orange pekoe tea bags

Blackberry Syrup (recipe follows)

¼ cup lemon juice

Blackberry-Mint Ice Cubes (recipe follows)

Orange wheels (optional)

In a medium saucepan, bring the water to a boil over high heat. Add the tea bags and remove from the heat. Cover and let stand 7 minutes.

Stir in the syrup, sweetening to taste, then cool completely, about 20 minutes. Place the flavored ice cubes in tall glasses and pour the tea over. Garnish each serving with an orange wheel, if desired.

BLACKBERRY SYRUP

MAKES 2 CUPS

1 cup granulated sugar

1 tablespoon grated lemon zest

1 tablespoon grated orange zest

6 whole cloves

1 cinnamon stick

2 cups water

12 ounces fresh blackberries

In a medium saucepan, combine the sugar, lemon and orange zests, cloves, cinnamon stick, and water. Bring to a boil over medium heat. Immediately add the berries and reduce the heat to low. Cover and simmer about 10 minutes. Remove from the heat and let stand 30 minutes.

Mash the berries in the syrup using a potato masher or the back of a wooden spoon. Pour the syrup through a fine-mesh sieve into a jar with a tight-fitting lid. Cover and refrigerate up to 2 weeks.

BLACKBERRY-MINT ICE CUBES

MAKES 28 STANDARD-SIZE ICE CUBES

½ cup fresh lemon juice

½ cup granulated sugar

¾ cup cold water

28 fresh blackberries (about 10 ounces)

28 small or medium fresh mint leaves

In a small bowl, stir together the lemon juice, sugar, and water until the sugar is dissolved. Place 1 blackberry in each section of two ice cube trays. Add a mint leaf to each cube, then carefully pour the lemon mixture into the cubes. Freeze until solid. Use the ice cubes with iced tea, lemonade, or punch.

PEACHY PUNCH

This sweet-tart alternative to the Bellini (page 102) is classic Southern refreshment, a hybrid drink that lands somewhere between a peach-flavored Arnold Palmer drink and a fruit puree. I wanted a fruit-forward beverage that hinted of tea, with less sugar than traditional sweet tea.

I started my search with a recipe in Bridgette A. Lacy's 2015 book, *Sunday Dinner: A Savor the South Cookbook*. Here, peach-flavored tea bags are sweetened with sugar, then flavored with peach nectar or peach-flavored juice drink. The tea is prepared early in the morning for a Sunday dinner later in the day so it has several hours to cool on the counter before being refrigerated, As Lacy, a former features and food writer for the *Raleigh News & Observer*, says, "Sometimes placing the tea in the refrigerator too soon can cause cloudiness."

I also was intrigued by a smoothie-like beverage in a 2008 cookbook by African American dietitian Sharon Hunt. Her *Bread from Heaven; or, A Collection of African-Americans' Home Cookin' and Somepin' Eat Recipes from Down in Georgia* offers a lean recipe, made with fresh peaches and without sugar. This appealed to me.

So, for the recipe that follows, I blitzed fresh, overripe peaches from the farmer's market to a smooth puree in a blender, then mixed in my homemade lemonade for tang. To give the drink the effervescence of a Bellini, you then stir in ginger ale, lemon-lime soda, or sparkling water—whichever appeals to you. SERVES 4

---

4 cups chopped pitted ripe peaches

3 cups water or brewed peach tea

1 cup Homemade Lemonade (page 210), chilled

Ginger ale, lemon-lime soda, or sparkling water

In a blender, combine the peaches and the water or tea. Blend until smooth. Pour into a large pitcher, cover, and refrigerate several hours, until thoroughly chilled.

Stir the lemonade into the peach mixture. Divide evenly among 4 Champagne flutes, then top off each drink with some ginger ale and serve.

ACKNOWLEDGMENTS

Writing a cookbook can be the fulfillment of a dream. It can also be a long, lonely, and arduous journey. Working on this project while onboarding at my new job as editor-in-chief of *Cook's Country* magazine, joining the cast of our television show, and restoring a historic hundred-year-old house during a pandemic amplified those tough realities. At times, it seemed impossible.

Thankfully, a faithful band of friends, family, colleagues, and supporters joined me in the process and helped turn the dream into a reality.

I am grateful to Alexandria Keller for your research and writing, for sorting and sifting through tons of information and bits of truth. You provided quotes, details, and obscure facts that gave the Black booze story a new and rich life.

Collaborating with Tiffanie Barriere, "the Drinking Coach," also was a gift. You are a force in the spirits world, but you shared your wisdom with tenderness and grace. I will forever treasure our give-and-take conversations and the knowledge we exchanged.

To my son, Brandon Tipton, and his sweet family, Whitney and Kylar: you were a blessing. Brandon, I appreciate your thoughtful tasting notes and the ways that you made the historic modern and relevant. You were more than that just my recipe tester; you shared behind-the-bar observations that spurred my curiosity. Thanks to you, Whitney, for storing boxes of liquor in your dining room with no end in sight. You're an amazing daughter.

I couldn't have completed this work without my brother, Derrick Hamilton, and sister-in-law, LaTanya Hamilton, who offered their kitchen and pantry when mine were buried in clouds of construction dust. I also treasure my husband Bruce Martin, my mom Beverly Hamilton, my niece Aliya, and my children, Jade, Christian, and Austin, who loved me through my anxieties as I balanced home, work, and travel.

I want to extend heartfelt thanks to all the creatives at *Cook's Country* who supported me when I was distracted. I'm also thankful for the wise and compassionate team at my agency, the Lisa Ekus Group. Lisa, Sally, and Jaimee, you never disappoint and always have my back.

I am eternally grateful to Clarkson Potter for once again assembling an incredible creative team that worked behind the scenes to make this dream come true. Thanks to Brittany Conerly for your spectacular photography, Kaitlin Wayne for the beautiful styling, Maeve Sheridan for your thoughtful prop selections, Marysarah Quinn for giving *Juice* its vibe and spirit, Darian Keels for keeping all the creative trains running on schedule, and Kristin Casemore and Brianne Sperber for ensuring that this book is in the hands of all its people.

Finally, I want to say a special thanks to my editor and my friend, Francis Lam. You listen when I am depleted and think I have nothing more to say, then you patiently extract more recipes and better stories from me, quietly refining them like an expert goldsmith. You nurture and nudge me along until I am holding a book in my hands that the ancestors and I can be proud of. I love you.

SELECTED BIBLIOGRAPHY

:::::

Here is a listing of all of the books I've referenced in the text and recipes—from self-published pamphlets to spiral-bound church volumes to lavishly illustrated trade works. Books from which I've drawn verbatim recipes are shown with their covers. The publications date from 1827 to the present, and I've included my own two previously published titles. I'm proud to have my books featured among such a richly diverse and remarkable collection.

ANDERSON, JULIAN
JULIAN'S RECIPES
1919

ANDERSON, SUNNY
Sunny's Kitchen: *Easy Food for Real Life*
2013

BAILEY, MASHAMA, and JOHN O. MORISANO
Black, White, and The Grey: *The Story of an Unexpected Friendship and a Beloved Restaurant*
2021

BARRETT, ANNA PEARL
Juneteenth: *Celebrating Freedom in Texas*
1999

BOOKER, JENNIFER
Field Peas to Foie Gras: *Southern Recipes with a French Accent*
2014

BULLOCK, TOM
The Ideal Bartender
1917

BURKE, HARMEN BURNEY
Burke's Complete Cocktail and Drinking Recipes
1934

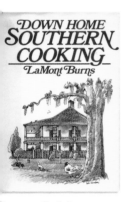

BURNS, LAMONT
Down Home Southern Cooking
1987

BUTLER, CLEORA
Cleora's Kitchens: *The Memoir of a Cook & Eight Decades of Great American Food*
1985

CATES, BEATRICE HIGHTOWER
Eliza's Cook Book: *Favorite Recipes Compiled by Negro Culinary Club of Los Angeles*
1936

CHANCE, JEANNE LOUISE DUZANT
Ma Chance's French Caribbean Creole Cooking
1985

CHILD, LYDIA MARIA
The American Frugal Housewife
1828

CITY FEDERATION OF COLORED WOMEN'S CLUBS
The Chef
1944

COOK, MAMIE
Work and Serve the Home: *Dedicated to the New Jersey Federation of Colored Women's Clubs*
1928

COUNCIL, MILDRED
Mama Dip's Kitchen
1999

DARDEN, NORMA JEAN
and CAROLE
**Spoonbread and
Strawberry Wine:**
Recipes and Reminiscences of a Family
1978; 25th edition 2003

DEKNIGHT, FREDA
A Date with a Dish: *A Cook
Book of American Negro Recipes*
1948

DELTA SIGMA THETA SORORITY
Occasions to Savor:
Our Meals, Menus and Memories
2004

DONALDSON, ENID
The Real Taste of Jamaica
2000

**East Austin Garden Club
Cookbook**
1990

ELDER, ROSE
Golfers Cookbook
1977

ELIE, LOLIS ERIC
Treme:
*Stories and Recipes from the Heart
of New Orleans*
2022

ESTES, RUFUS
Good Things to Eat
As Suggested by Rufus
1911

FERGUSON, SHEILA
Soul Food: *Classic Cuisine
from the Deep South*
1994

FISHER, ABBY
What Mrs. Fisher Knows About Old Southern Cooking
1881

Food for My Household:
Recipes by Members of Ebenezer Baptist Church
1986

GANT, BESSIE M.
Bess Gant's Cook Book:
Over 600 Original Recipes
1947

GOINS, JOHN B.
The American Waiter
1914

GOURDET, GREGORY AND JJ GOODE
Everyone's Table: *Global Recipes for Modern Health*
2021

GRAY, JON, PIERRE SERRAO, AND LESTER WALKER
Ghetto Gastro Presents Black Power Kitchen
2022

GUILLORY, QUEEN IDA
Cookin' with Queen Ida:
Bon Temps Creole Recipes (and Stories) from the Queen of Zydeco Music
1990

HALL, CARLA
Carla Hall's Soul Food:
Everyday and Celebration
2018

HALL, TAMIKA, WITH COLIN ASARE-APPIAH
Black Mixcellence:
A Comprehensive Guide to Black Mixology
2022

Hamilton Hall Cookbook
1947

HARRIS, DUNSTAN A.
Island Cooking:
Recipes from the Caribbean
1988

HARRIS, JESSICA B.
The Africa Cookbook:
Tastes of a Continent
2010

HARRIS, JESSICA B.
Rum Drinks: *50 Caribbean Cocktails, from Cuba Libre to Rum Daisy*
2010

HARRIS, JESSICA B.
Sky Juice and Flying Fish:
Traditional Caribbean Cooking
1991

HASSAN, HAWA
In Bibi's Kitchen
2020

HENDERSON, JEFF, WITH RAMIN GANESHRAM
America I AM:
Pass It Down Cookbook
2011

HOLDREDGE, HELEN
Mammy Pleasant's Cookbook
1970

HOLLAND, TANYA
Brown Sugar Kitchen:
New-Style, Down-Home Recipes from Sweet West Oakland
2014

HUNT, SHARON
Bread from Heaven:
Or, A Collection of African-American Home Cookin' and Somepin' Eat Recipes from Down in Georgia
2008

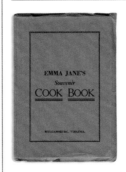

JACKSON, EMMA JANE
Emma Jane's Souvenir Cook Book
1937

JENKINS, CHARLOTTE
Gullah Cuisine:
By Land and By Sea
2020

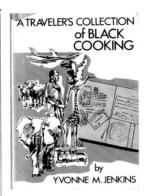

JENKINS, YVONNE M.
A Traveler's Collection of Black Cooking
1994

JOHNSON, JJ, and ALEXANDER SMALLS
Between Harlem and Heaven: *Afro-Asian-American Cooking for Big Nights, Weekends, and Every Day*
2018

LACY, BRIDGETTE A.
Sunday Dinner:
A Savor the South Cookbook
2015

LEWIS, EDNA, and SCOTT PEACOCK
The Gift of Southern Cooking: *Recipes and Revelations from Two Great American Cooks*
2003

LEWIS, EDNA
The Taste of Country
Cooking
1976

LYNCH, CARRIE PAULINE
Pauline's Practical Book of
the Culinary Art for Clubs,
Home or Hotels
1919

MAHAMMITT, SARAH HELEN
Recipes and Domestic
Service:
The Mahammitt School of Cookery
1939

MAISONET, ILLYANNA
Diasporican:
A Puerto Rican Cookbook
2022

MCQUEEN, ADELE BOLDEN
West African Cooking for
Black American Families
1982

MEACHAM, SARAH HAND
Every Home a Distillery:
Alcohol, Gender, and Technology
in the Colonial Chesapeake
2009

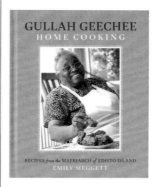

MEGGETT, EMILY
Gullah Geechee Home
Cooking:
Recipes from the Matriarch
of Edisto Island
2022

MILLER, KLANCY
Cooking Solo:
The Joy of Cooking for Yourself
2020

Mr. Boston: Official
Bartender's Guide
50th Edition
1984

MUNSON, BESSIE
Bless the Cook
1980

MUSTIPHER, SHANNON
Tiki: Modern Tropical Cocktails
2019

NATIONAL COUNCIL OF
NEGRO WOMEN
The Historical Cookbook
of the American Negro:
The Classic Yearlong Celebration of
Black Heritage from Emancipation
Proclamation Breakfast Cake to
Wandering Pilgrim's Stew
1958; 2000 reprint

NATIONAL COUNCIL OF
NEGRO WOMEN
Mother Africa's Table:
*A Collection of West African and
African American Recipes and
Cultural Traditions*
1998

NATIONAL COUNCIL OF
NEGRO WOMEN
**Favorite Recipes from
Our Best Cooks**
1982

NEELY, PAT and GINA
**Down Home with the
Neelys:** *A Southern Family
Cookbook*
2009

NMAAHC
**Sweet Home Café
Cookbook**
2018

O'MEARA, MALLORY
Girly Drinks
2021

ORTIZ, YVONNE
A Taste of Puerto Rico
1997

OSSEO-ASARE, FRAN
**A Good Soup Attracts
Chairs:** *A First African Cookbook
for American Kids*
1993

PARKER, CURTIS
The Lost Art of Scratch Cooking:
*Recipes from the Kitchen of
Natha Adkins Parker*
1997

PEYTON, ATHOLENE
The Peytonia Cook Book
1906

QUESTLOVE
Mixtape Potluck:
*A Dinner Party for Friends, Their
Recipes, and the Songs They Inspire*
2019

RAIFORD, MATTHEW
Bress 'n' Nyam: *Gullah
Geechee Recipes from a
Sixth-Generation Farmer*
2021

REDMAN, DAISY
**Four Great Southern
Cooks**
1980

RICHARD, LENA
**Lena Richard's New
Orleans Cook Book**
1939

RICHARDS, TODD
Soul: *A Chef's Culinary
Evolution in 150 Recipes*
2018

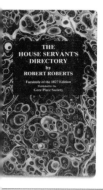

ROBERTS, ROBERT
The House Servant's Directory
1827

ROBINSON, SALLIE ANN
Cooking the Gullah Way:
Morning, Noon & Night
2007

RUSSELL, MALINDA
A Domestic Cook Book
1866

HUSSEY, DOROTHY SHANKLIN
Forty Years in the Kitchen
1983

SAMUELSSON, MARCUS
The Red Rooster Cookbook
2016

SAMUELSSON, MARCUS
The Rise: *Black Cooks and
the Soul of American Food*
2020

SCOTT, ELLE SIMONE
Boards: *Stylish Spreads for
Casual Gatherings*
2022

SMALLS, ALEXANDER
Meals, Music, and Muses:
*Recipes from My African American
Kitchen*
2020

SMART-GROSVENOR, VERTAME
Vibration Cooking:
*Or, The Traveling Notes of
a Geechee Girl*
2011

SMITH, BARBARA "B."
**B. Smith Cooks
Southern Style**
2011

SMITH, LUCILLE BISHOP
**Lucille's Treasure Chest
of Fine Foods**
1941

SNOOP DOGG
From Crook to Cook:
*Platinum Recipes from
Tha Boss Dogg's Kitchen*
2018

SPRUILL, MRS. J. F., AND
MRS. STOKES ADDERTON OF
THE SOROSIS CLUB, EDS.
Paynie's Parties:
*A Collection of Party Recipes from
Mrs. Jessie Hargrave Payne of
Lexington N.C., Tested and Proven*
1955

SOUTH CENTRAL DISTRICT RED
CROSS, LOS ANGELES CHAPTER
**Favorite Recipes for
Everyone**
1981

STARR, KATHY
**The Soul of Southern
Cooking**
1989

TATE, BIBBY, and
ETHEL DIXON
**Colorful Louisiana Cuisine
in Black and White**
1990

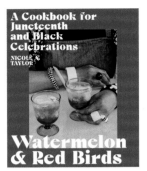

TAYLOR, NICOLE
**Watermelon and
Red Birds:** *A Cookbook for
Juneteenth and Black Celebrations*
2022

TERRY, BRYANT
Black Food: *Stories, Art,
and Recipes from Across the
African Diaspora*
2021

TERRY, BRYANT
The Inspired Vegan
2012

THIAM, PIERRE
The Fonio Cookbook:
An Ancient Grain Rediscovered
2019

TILLERY, CAROLYN QUICK
**The African-American
Heritage Cookbook:**
*Traditional Recipes & Fond
Memories from Alabama's
Renowned Tuskegee Institute*
2001

TILLERY, CAROLYN QUICK
**Southern Homecoming
Traditions**
2006

TIPTON-MARTIN, TONI
The Jemima Code:
*Two Centuries of African American
Cookbooks*
2015

TIPTON-MARTIN, TONI
Jubilee: *Recipes from Two
Centuries of African American
Cooking*
2019

T-PAIN
Can I Mix You a Drink?
*50 Cocktails from My Life
and Career*
2021

TURNER, BERTHA L.
The Federation Cook Book
*A Collection of Tested Recipes,
Contributed by the Colored Women
of the State of California*
1910; reissued 2018

Watts, Edith and John
Jesse's Book of Creole and Deep South Recipes
1954

West, Rebecca
Rebecca's Cookbook
1942

Williams, Caroline Randall, and Alice Randall
Soul Food Love
2015

Williams, Milton
The Party Book
1981

Williams, Miss R. Omosunlola
Miss Williams' Cookery Book
1957

Willinsky, Helen
Jerk Barbecue from Jamaica
2007

Wilson, Ellen Gibson
A West African Cook Book: *An Introduction of Good Food from Ghana, Liberia, Nigeria and Sierra Leone with Recipes Collected and Adapted by Ellen Gibson Wilson*
1971

Wilson, Melba
Melba's American Comfort: *100 Recipes from My Heart to Your Kitchen*
2021

Wondrich, Dave
How to Make Old Kentucky Famed Drinks
1934

Woods, Marvin
The New Low-Country Cooking: *125 Recipes for Coastal Southern Cooking with Innovative Style*
2000

MEASUREMENTS & EQUIVALENTS

The recipes in this book, as in most cocktail books, use fluid ounces as the standard measurement for liquor. While preparing drinks, bartenders traditionally use a jigger, the basic two-cupped stainless-steel measuring device. The larger cup measures out exactly 1 jigger, or $1\frac{1}{2}$ ounces. The smaller cup is normally $\frac{1}{2}$ jigger, or $\frac{3}{4}$ ounce. A shot glass is also $1\frac{1}{2}$ ounces. A jigger or shot glass is a must for any home bar, but if you don't have either of these tools handy, use the equivalents chart on the opposite page. Measurements should always be level unless directed otherwise.

⅛ teaspoon = 1 dash = 0.5 mL

¼ teaspoon = 2 dashes = 1 mL

½ teaspoon = 4 dashes = 2.5 mL

1 teaspoon = ⅓ tablespoon = 5 mL

1½ teaspoons = 1 bar spoon = 7.5 mL

1 tablespoon = 2 bar spoons = ½ fluid ounce = 15 mL

2 tablespoons = ⅛ cup = 1 fluid ounce = 30 mL

3 tablespoons = 1 jigger = 1½ fluid ounces = 45 mL

4 tablespoons = ¼ cup = 2 fluid ounces = 60 mL

5⅓ tablespoons = ⅓ cup = 2¾ fluid ounces = 80 mL

6 tablespoons = 2 jiggers = 3 fluid ounces = 90 mL

8 tablespoons = ½ cup = 4 fluid ounces = 120 mL

10⅔ tablespoons = ⅔ cup = 5 fluid ounces = 160 mL

12 tablespoons = ¾ cup = 6 fluid ounces = 180 mL

16 tablespoons = 1 cup = 8 fluid ounces = 240 mL

GLOSSARY OF GLASSES

LOWBALLS · ROCKS

FOOTED ROCKS
COSMOPOLITAN

SNIFTER

COUPE

MARGARITA

MARTINI

MILKSHAKE

IRISH COFFEEE

CORDIALS

SHOT

SHOOTER

CHAMPAGNE
FLUTE

CHAMPAGNE
COUPE

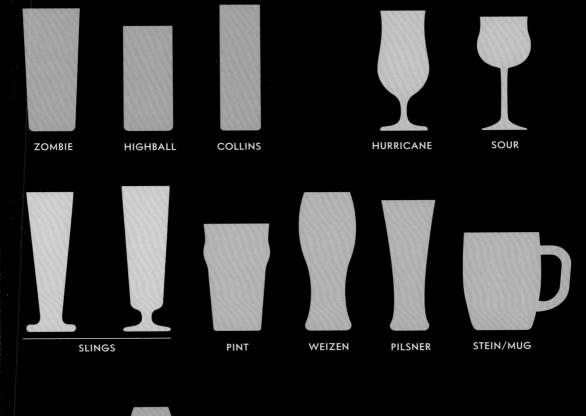

ZOMBIE HIGHBALL COLLINS HURRICANE SOUR

SLINGS PINT WEIZEN PILSNER STEIN/MUG

RED WHITE BALLOON WINE TASTING SHERRY GOBLET

SUBJECT INDEX

RECIPE INDEX

ABOUT THE AUTHOR

TONI TIPTON-MARTIN

is a culinary journalist, a community activist,
the editor-in-chief of *Cook's Country* magazine,
and the author of two James Beard Award–
winning books, *The Jemima Code* and *Jubilee*.
Her collection of more than 450 African
American cookbooks has been exhibited at the
James Beard House, and she has twice been
invited to participate in First Lady Michelle
Obama's programs to raise a healthier
generation of kids. She is a founding
member of the Southern Foodways
Alliance and Foodways Texas.

CLARKSON POTTER is a
trademark and POTTER with
colophon is a registered trademark
of Penguin Random House LLC.

Library of Congress Cataloging-in-
Publication Data
Identifiers: LCCN 2023005867
(print) | LCCN 2023005868 (ebook)
Classification: LCC TX951 .T498
2023 (print) | LCC TX951 (ebook)
| DDC 641.87/40973—dc23/
eng/20230317
LC record: lccn.loc.gov/2023005867
LC ebook record: lccn.loc.gov/
2023005868

Printed in China

Editor: Francis Lam
Editorial assistant: Darian Keels
Designer: Marysarah Quinn
Production editor: Mark McCauslin
Production manager: Jessica Heim
Compositors: Merri Ann Morrell
    and Hannah Hunt
Copyeditor: Carole Berglie
Proofreader: Andrea Peabbles
Indexer: Ken DellaPenta
Food Stylist: Kaitlin Wayne
Prop Stylist: Maeve Sheridan
Publicist: Kristin Casemore
Marketer: Brianne Sperber
Drink silhouettes:
    iStock/Berezka_Klo

10 9 8 7 6 5 4 3 2 1

First Edition